Quips, Rips
&
Provocative Questions

by Caleb Spalding Atwood

Dorrance Publishing Co
585 Alpha Drive
Pittsburgh, PA 15238
Visit our website at *www.dorrancebookstore.com*

ISBN: 978-1-6442-6606-9
eISBN:978-1-6442-6626-7

Quips, Rips & Provocative Questions

by Caleb Spalding Atwood

DORRANCE PUBLISHING CO
EST. 1920
PITTSBURGH, PENNSYLVANIA 15238

INTRODUCTION

Collecting and Creating quips, rips and provocative questions has been nearly a decades-long fascination that led to the *Quip Factory* in 2010 that *ForWord Clarion Reviews* rated five stars out of five and opined:

> *"Quip Factory* is a pleasure to peruse, and every page offers another surprising opportunity to manipulate (some say "mutilate") the English Language in new and witty ways. From writers to public speakers to anyone with a passion for Language and a desire to entertain themselves and others, Atwood's book is a must have."

In it, a reviewer chimed in with:

> *"Quip Factory: Millions of Quips, Rips, Dingers, Zingers, and Barbs, and How You Can Create Even More"* written by Caleb Spalding Atwood, is a must-have reference for writers, would-be comedians, and even the average Joe who wants to "bring about a barrel of belly laughs at the next social gathering."

Returning to earth, most people seem to think "quip" is simply a synonym for "joke". That's understandable because "quip" is defined as a "witty or sarcastic remark," and "joke" as something "amusing or comical." Both are based upon things that are unexpected, and as old time comedian W.C. Fields put it, **"It seems people only laugh at the unexpected."** Actually, a good case can be made for defining humorous or funny themselves as "unexpected". Quips and rips differ in that the objective of jokes is to get laughs, whereas the objective of quips is to express opinions that are or may be a bit bitter, bizarre, clever, curious, droll, eccentric, odd, sarcastic or witty characterizations, remarks or opinions that tease, taunt, shock or denigrate individuals or entities that richly deserve such "recognition". Even then, they'll often get laughs.

Belittling, for example, is richly deserved when putting down bought-and paid-for politicians, corruption, the mafia, negative interest rates, racial bias, voter fraud, war, or anything dishonest, despicable, stupid, or criminal. Unfortunately, criticism is often laced with profanity that often reflects at least as poorly on those using it as it does on their targets. With few exceptions, expressing opinions with profanity-free quips, rips, or provocative questions is less offensive and more effective and even humorous.

Quips enable us to say a great deal quickly as illustrated in these examples in Ambrose Bierce's brilliant satirical interpretation of English words style. Examples, with many more soon to follow.

Coleman Young:	"Sir, I'll have you know, all racial stereotypes are not wrong." (Response by former black mayor of Detroit when a critic said he should be hung.)

    Caleb Spalding Atwood

Debt:	Slavery of the free. (Pubilious Syrus)
Penny saved:	Congressional oversight. (Hal Lee Luyah)
Zimbabwe:	Federal Reserve role model.

A good way to respond to something inane, insane, adverse, per-verse, weird, wild, or worse, is by equating it with something are even more so in a quip, rip or provocative question. That's because quips, etc. tend to be controversial, and controversy has journalistic sex appeal. Imagine the ink and air a commentator would get if he or she were to say things like "Automatic toilets flush when Hillaryous speaks" or "X has taken the cure for sobriety."

Opinions expressed in this book range from mildly to wildly controversial, so you are bound to find at least a few (dozen?) you find offensive. That should not be a problem however, because you'll also find boatloads of ways to refute or put down virtually any such opinion. To illustrate, if you disagree with the following adaptation of a quip by the noted British historian Thomas Babington Macaulay,

> "A man who has never been in the tropics does not know what a thunderstorm means; a man who has never looked on Niagara or waded through a rush hour thunderstorm in NY City, has but a faint idea of a cataract;"

Unfortunately, many quips and contrasts like "as different as apples and oranges," "higher than a kite," "quick as a wink," etc., have been around so long and used so extensively that they have lost their cutting edge and become what Oliver Wendell Holms senior called "verbacide" - (aka Quipicide). That should not be a burden for you as we proceed..

Timely quips tend to be most effective, but older quips often have staying power. Attorney and blogger, Jim Karger came up with a classic when president Obama was awarded the Nobel Peace Prize prior to being elected. Karger compared that with a bank offering new customers **"either a toaster or a Nobel Peace Prize"** and followed with **"Unfortunately, they were out of toasters."**

We will be working with words, but incongruity (i.e., things that are unexpected) can even make people laugh at music. According to "Literary Devices" via the internet, "...quips, rips and provocative questions are satirical devices employed by writers, speakers and entertainers using humor to expose, criticize and castigate foolishness and corruption of individuals, organizations, governments or societies."

Unless your age borders on Methuselah's, you are not likely to remember outstanding examples of this by Spike Jones, a hugely popular American band leader decades ago whose "music" thrived on the unexpected - dissonance, barking dogs, cars crashing, explosions, shrieks, screams, thunder, bells ringing, horns honking, etc. - and sounded suspiciously like congress.

In addition to hundreds of quips and rips that follow, there are opinions expressed in the form of provocative questions. Although seldom thought of as such, questions can often be effective vehicles for expressing opinions, quickly and cleverly, as you will find in abundance in chapter VI - Provocative Questions.

Herein when someone is quoted exactly or very close to it, their name follows in parenthesis - (Mark Twain), etc. When

Caleb Spalding Atwood

there is some doubt about who authored a quip, there is a question mark next to their name - (P.J. O'Rourke?), etc.. Slightly altered comments or quips have tildes in front of their names (~W.C. Fields). When I cannot recall who authored a quote and don't want to take "credit" for it, it is followed by "(?)"

NOTE: If you are not completely satisfied with this book, you may get your money back. All you need do is to sell it it to someone else.

CHAPTER I

BIERCE QUIPS

Ambrose Bierce, born in 1842, has been heralded as a brilliant, biting and, at times, bizarre critic who worked his way up from a printer's apprentice to editor of William Randolph Hearst's *San Francisco Examiner*. During his career he became one of the most influential journalists on the west coast, often butchering hypocrites, opportunists, politicians, racketeers, and others worthy of it, with quips. His major works are in *The Collected Writings of Ambrose Bierce*, introduced by Clifton Fadiman, who opined:

> "Bierce will remain one of our most interesting and eccentric figures in our literature, one of the greatest wits, one of our most improvising satirists…a writer one cannot casually pass by."

A few his quips are included for flavor among others in his style that follow.

2016 Election: Mainstream media v. Trump.

Abortion control: Clinics with two-year waiting lists.

Abortion: If men could get pregnant, abortion would be a sacrament.
(Florence Kennedy)

Absence: Common cure for love. (Lord Byron)

Accident: 'The greatest of all inventors."
(Mark Twain)

Acquaintance: Degree of friendship called slight when it's object is poor or obscure and intimate when he or she is rich or famous.

Adult: Superannuated adolescent.

Advantage: To get it, take it. (Georg Eliot.)

Advertising[1]:   Putting mascara on maggots.

Advertising[2]:   Rattling a stick inside a swill bucket.
(George Orwell)

Advice: Words that go in ears and disappear.

Agreement: Made more precious by disagreement.
(Publicis's Syrus)

Alan Greenspan: "If my words seem clear, then obviously there has been a misunderstanding."

Alibi[1]:   Spontaneous obfuscation.

Alibi[2]:   I was doing push-ups - and someone slid a woman under me.

Alimony[1]:   Paying you're sorry.

      Caleb Spalding Atwood

Alimony[2]:	The love of an ex-wife's life.
Alliance:	Union of two thieves who have their hands so deeply inserted in each other's pocket that they cannot separately plunder a third. (Bierce)
Alliteration:	Reason beetle, bat, bumblebee or baboon in one's bonnet sounds better than flamingo, spider or Tsetse fly.
Alone:	In bad company. (Bierce)
Amateur:	College athlete under an assumed name.
Ambassadorship:	Quid pro campaign contribution.
Ambidextrous:	Able to pick pockets with either hand.
Ambition[1]:	High octane egomania.
Ambition[2]:	Enemy of peace. (John Cowper Powys)
America[1]:	Great country where even an undocumented alien can become president.
America[2]:	Subversion of many for the benefit of the few. (?)
America[3]:	"The only country that has gone from barbarism to degeneration without the usual interval of civilization." (~ Georges Clemenceau)
Ancestors:	To forget them is to be a brook with-

out a source, a tree without a root. (Chinese proverb)

Apes: Descendants from man?

Appropriate: "Steal" in DC.

April 1st: Ideal day for election.

Art[1]:   "Not a mirror to reflect the world, but a hammer with which to shape it." (Vladimir Nabokov)

Art[2]:   The only way to run away without leaving home. (Twyla Tharp)

Assange: Founder of Wikipedia and proof America will not tolerate truth.

Assassination: "Extreme censorship." (George Bernard Shaw)

Atheist plea: "So help me Hades."

Atheist: Person with no invisible means of support. (John Buhon)

Attractive: Rich.

Atwood's Law: Treat people like dogs and they'll treat you like a Fire hydrant.

Author unknown: By billions.

Autobiography[1]:   "Obituary with last installment missing." (Quentin Crisp)

Autobiography[2]:   "**Alibi**ography." (~ Charles Lamb)

Automation: Job killer for many, blessing for far more.

Bacchus: Convenient deity invented by the ancients as an excuse for getting drunk. (Bierce)

Bach: "Second rate composer"- hired after two most famous refused a job.

Bachelor: Man who wouldn't take "yes" for an answer.

Bachelorette: Woman who hasn't made the same mistake once. (?)

Bail-ins: Reverse Robin Hoods.

Bailouts: Plunder of poor to protect prosperous.

Balanced diet: Caffeine, sugar, fat and alcohol - aka Irish coffee. (?)

Bald: Unable to afford Trump's hairdresser.

Bald-faced lie: Perfidious prevarication.

Ban: Promote.

Bank: "A place that will lend you money – if you prove you do not need it." (Bob Hope)

Banker bonuses: Hush money.

Banker: Fellow who will loan you his umbrella - if it isn't raining. (~Mark Twain)

Bankers: In bed with the Fed – or vice versa?

Bankers' Goal: Crash cash, so even beggars need accounts they can bail in.

Bankruptcy: When a balance sheet won't.

Banks: "Easier to rob by setting up, than holding up." (Bertold Brecht)

Banksters: Big enough to bail, too big to jail.

Barack: Drone-prone president.

Bargains: Millions of Americans can now save money on gas they no longer need to drive to jobs they no longer can afford to have.

Beauty: Is only sin deep. (Saki)

Beheading: Reward for criticizing monarchy.

Belladonna: In Italian a beautiful lady. In English a deadly poison - a striking example of the essential identity of the two tongues. (Bierce)

Berate: Eviscerate, humiliate or castigate to the best of one's hostility.

Betrayed: Individuals whose campaign contribution did not pay off.

     Caleb Spalding Atwood

Better: Enemy of good. (Voltaire)

Biden: Plagiarizer extraordinaire forced to re-take a course in college because of it.

Bigamy[1]: "One wife too many - same as monogamy." (~ Oscar Wilde)

Bigamy[2]: Extramarital matrimony.

Bi-lingual: Equally adept at English and profanity.

Bill and Hillary: Beneficiaries of Clinton Charitable Foundation.

Birthday greeting: "Happy B-day, hope you're enjoying your life as much as you have helped millions of others enjoy theirs." (Greeting to Charles Kimbrough, anchor man on Murphy Brown TV show, on his 80th.

Blyth Masters: Set record by being appointed and dis-appointed to Commodities Trading Commission in a single day.

Body-snatchers: Robbers who supply young med students with what old physicians used to supply undertakers. (?)

Bogus Statistic: Inflation below 2%.

Booby trap: No money down.

Boomerang: Weapon for masochists.

Booze: Cure for common sense.

Booze[1]:   Makes a man feel like a twenty year old
                          - maybe even two.

Booze[2]:   Cure for sobriety.

Boring: Triple Van Winkle.

Borrower: Servant to the lender. (Proverb)

Boss: Spouse. (Female variety).

Bottled air: Pollution solution.

Brag: Prevaricate.

Brain surgery: "Easier than getting elected." (Dr. Ben
                          Carson?)

Brain transplants: Remedy for people with sub-zero IQ's –
                          aka incumbents

Brainwash: "Educate" in advertising.

Breathtaking: Beheading.

Brevity: The sole of wit. (Shakespeare)

Bribe: Campaign contribution – aka political
                          perk or pork.

Bribery: Road to success in US?

Bribes[1]:   World's most profitable investments.

Bribes[2]:   Reason politicians vote for loopy laws?

                        Caleb Spalding Atwood

Bride: Woman with prospects of happiness behind her. (Bierce)

British: "Have the most rigid code of immorality in the world." (Malcolm Bradbury)

Broken engagement: Near Mrs.

BS: Converts candidates into incumbents.

Bucky Fuller: Inventor of geodesic igloo.

Bull: Derives from Dutch word for "lover."

Bullfights: Fund raisers for American Society for Prevention of Cruelty to Animals. (?)

Bully: Could have beaten Muhammad Ali with both hands tied behind his back. (i.e. Ali's)

Burning Question[1]:   Do laughing hyenas have a sense of humor?

Burning Question[2]:   Why is it that those who can least afford it, have the most - babies?

Burning Question[3]:   Would baseball be the national pastime if not for steroids?

Burning Question[4]:   Can X possibly be as young as he/she acts?

Burning Question[5]:   Why are all hurricanes named after women?

Burning Question[6]: How long will it be before passports are required to get in and out of California?

Busy People: Get things done that others don't have time for. (Elbert Hubbard)

Buxom: Silicone show-off.

Buy Car: Create jobs - for robots.

Campaign contribution: Down payment. (Orwell)

C Students: "Rulers of the world." (Harry Truman)

Calamity: Misfortune for ourselves, good fortune for others. (?)

Calexico: nee California.

Canadian Club: Hockey stick. (groan)

"Cancer cured." AMA Journal announcement in 1888. (*Flood your body with Oxygen* by Ed McCabe.

Cancer research: Search for profitable alternative to water to cure cancer that cannot survive in highly oxygenated tissue. (~ Ed McCabe)

Cancer: Cure for smoking.

Candid: Insulting.

Capitalism: Dictatorship under assumed name.

　　　　Caleb Spalding Atwood

Ceasefire: Calm before the norm.

Censor: Generate interest.

CFTC: Federal watchdog created to protect financial predators from their prey.

Champagne: "Better than a lie detector when seeking truth." (~Graham Greene)

Chance of rain: Bring ark.

Chastity: "The most unnatural of sexual perversions." (Aldus Huxley)

Chicken hawk: Cowardly warmonger.

Citizen: Government ATM.

City: Concrete zoo. (Desmond Morris)

Classic: "A book people praise, but do not read." (Mark Twain)

Clear conscience: Faulty memory.

Cocaine: Cure for competence.

Cocktails: Cure for cancer because it cannot survive in alcohol?

Collaborate: Capitulate in DC.

Collateral carnage: Women and children killed by drones.

College: "Pays, if you're a good open-field runner." (Will Rogers)

Colorado: Where politicians either smoke too much, or not enough, pot.

Commandment: Thou Shalt Not Commit Monogamy. (Bill Clinton?)

Commencement: Entre to unemployment.

Committees: Where ideas go to die.

Common enemy: "Reason kids and grandparents get along so well." (Sam Levinson)

Common sense: Whatever we agree with.

Complain: "People who cease to complain, cease to think." (Napoleon)

Compliment: "You've been more than kind and I certainly do depreciate it." ("Compliment" I received.)

Conceit: "God's gift to little men." (Bruce Barton)

Concrete cloverleaf: Our national flower. (Lewis Mumford)

Confidant: One entrusted by A with the secrets of B confided to him by C. (Bierce)

Congress[1]: "Three of the seven wonders of the world combined cost less than one office building for 200 congressmen." (David Brinkley)

Congress[2]: Life imitating comedy - or vice versa?

 Caleb Spalding Atwood

Congress[3]:   "The only Native American criminal class." (Mark Twain)

Congress[4]:   Where consensus and common sense seldom collide. (?)

Congressmen: Bankster lapdogs.

Consensus: Mutual misunderstanding.

Consent decree: Where stock manipulators insist they've done nothing wrong, but promise never again to do what they claim never to have done. (~ *How I cracked the Alpha Code* by Jim Roberts)

Conservative: A statesman who is enamored of existing evils, as distinguished from the Liberal who wishes to replace them with others. (Bierce)

Consistent: Reliably incompetent.

Constitutional: Irrelevant.

Contagious: Prevarication in politics.

Contemporary Ed: "Wake me up if I'm studying." (Calvin R. Haywood)

Contribution[1]:   Fine for crime payable in advance.

Contribution[2]:   Down payment.

Cooperate: Capitulate in D.C.

Courageous:	Afraid to retreat.
Curfews:	Laws that prevent kids from acting like adults.
Cowardice:	Protection against temptation. (Mark Twain)
CPAs:	High paid professionals who get answers to tough tax questions from the internet.
Crazy:	Sub-abnormal.
Criminal:	Profitable.
Critic:	Commentator with fine toothed axe.
Criticism:	"Never inhibited by ignorance." (Harold McMillan)
Criticizing others:	Dishonest way of praising ourselves. (~ Will Durant)
Critics:	Scribes who love to write about things they hate.
Curfews:	Laws intended to prevent kids from acting like adults.
Cynic:	A scoundrel who sees things as they are rather than as they ought to be. (?)
Debriefed:	Nude.
Debt[1]:	An ingenious substitute for the chain and whip of the slave-driver. (Bierce)

 Caleb Spalding Atwood

Debt[2]:   Slavery of the free. (Pubilious Syrus)

Deep State: "Deep-six" for freedom.

Delegate: Spread blame.

Deliberate: Pretend to decide.

Delicacy: Kentucky fried buzzard.

Democracy[1]:   When citizens lose money on sane investment, citizens pay. When government loses money on insane investments, citizens pay.

Democracy[2]:   Subversion of the many for the benefit of the few – banksters.

Democracy[3]:   On the brink - of being extinct.

Democracy[4]:   Wolves and a lamb deciding what to have for lunch. (Bierce)

Depressions: Perilous periods when guns must be banned to protect politicians responsible for perilous periods.

Derriere-ship: Leadership from behind.

Desperate need: Unemployed politicians.

Detroit: City so poor half of the prostitutes are virgins. (?)

Diagnosis: A physician's forecast of disease by patient's pulse and purse. (Bierce)

Diet:

Endeavor to prevent food from going to waist.

Diplomacy[1]:

Saying the nastiest things in the nicest way

Diplomacy[2]:

The patriotic art of lying for your country. (Bierce)

Diplomat:

"Person who thinks twice before saying nothing." (Frederick Sawyer)

Discretion:

Separating sane from insane and embracing the latter. (?)

Discrimination:

Where decency fears to tread.

Distance:

"The only thing rich are willing for the poor to call theirs, and keep." (Bierce)

Divorce:

Miscarriage of marriage.

Drinking:

Pause from thinking. (Lord Byron)

Driver education:

Accidents.

Drone[1]:

Killing device used to save lives.

Drone[2]:

Successor to boots on the ground.

Drone[3]:

Modern day Kamikaze.

E-commerce:

Easy way to give criminals access to your bank account. (~ James Napoli)

Economic forecast:

Financial guesstimate

Edited:	Fact-scratched. (?)
Education:	Progressive discovery of our own ignorance. (Will Durant)
Egotism[1]:	Case of mistaken nonentity. (Barbara Stanwyck)
Egotism[2]:	Doing NY Times Sunday crossword puzzle with a pen. (~Bierce)
Egotist:	"Person of low taste, more interested in himself than in me." (Bierce)
Egregious theft:	Bankster bail-ins.
Elastic statistics:	Murder rates heavily weighted with gangsters killed by other gangsters.
Election[1]:	contests between current and aspiring incompetents.
Elections[2]:	Proof most voters can be fooled most of the time.
Elections[2]:	Heads elite win, tails citizens lose.
Élite:	Political puppet masters.
Employed:	People whose unemployment benefits have run out - according to US Bureau of Labor Standards.
End Speeding:	Handmade "Speed Trap Ahead" sign. (worked for me.)

Enemy: Any country, group or individual the international banking cartel cannot control.

English[1]:   Rapidly becoming US second language.

ENRONerate: Swindle.

EPA Goal: Keep coal in a hole.

Equality: "Women who seek to be equal with men lack ambition." (Timothy Leary)

Error: Terror minus "T."

Ethical: Undetected.

Exceptions: To everything except death, taxes and politics.

Exile: Refuge for whistleblowers.

Exit: Entry for another. (~ Tom Stoppard)

Experience: Synonym for "mistake." (?)

Explanation: Alibi.

Extinct: Privacy.

Face lift: No problem for (name person) because he/she has two.

Fact free repartee: Politically correct.

Failure[1]:   "Good and gracious loser." (Knute Rockne, former Notre Dame football coach)

                      Caleb Spalding Atwood

Failure[2]: "The condiment that gives success its flavor." (Truman Capote)

Faith in the Fed: Disappearing act.

Fake News: Anything supporting the deep state.

Familiarity: "Breeds attempt." (Goodman Ace)

Familiarize: Strip search

Fanatic: "One who won't change his mind and won't change the subject." (Winston Churchill)

Fatal alternatives: Republicans, Democrats, Independents..

Fate: "Whatever limits us." (Ralph Waldo Emerson)

Fear: Only motivation greater than greed.

Fed[1]: Bankster lap dog.

Fiat[1]: Italian auto, US dollar.

Fiat[2]: Purchaser of American taxpayers' bailed-out Chrysler 290.

Financial plunder: Negative interest rates.

Fired: Napalmed.

Fix: If the fix was in for Hillary, the fix needs fixing.

Firing Squad: Ultimate deterrent.

Fiscal insanity:	Negative interest rates.
Fiscal sanity:	Extinct since repeal of 1933 Glass-Steagall banking act.
Flattery:	"All right, so long as you don't inhale." (Adlai Stevenson, former governor of Illinois.)
Fool's gold:	Paper gold (aka futures contracts).
Foot in Mouth:	Ubiquitous political infirmity.
Football coach:	Highest paid faculty member.
Forecast:	Premeditated hunch.
Foreign policy:	aka "moron policy."
Forgetfulness:	Evidence of lost youth.
Foundations:	Entities that make bribes deductible.
FOX News:	Fair, balanced and unafraid, except when reporting manipulation of precious metals prices.
FOX on the Run:	Liberals favorite bluegrass song.
Free advice:	Expensive.
Free market:	Where "investors" sell gold or silver they do not have to crash their prices and then buy them back profitably.
Free press:	Kind remembrance.

 Caleb Spalding Atwood

Free speech[1]:	Imperiled by Fake News.
Free speech[2]:	Tolerable – when mainstream media agrees.
Freedom:	Imperiled without privacy, free speech, decent jobs and impartial media.
Friendship:	A ship big enough to carry two in fair weather, but only one in foul. (Bierce)
Frightened:	Cognizant.
Frightening:	"When a doctor tells you you're as healthy as a dollar." (Ronald Reagan)
Gaffe:	"When a politician tells the truth." (~ Michael Kinsley)
Gay Marriage:	Birth control.
Gigantic:	Medium after inflation.
Goal of Quips:	To get people laughing with rather than at you.
Goals:	Republicans: create jobs. Democrats: dump Trump.
God:	Deity who damns things for you.
Gold and Silver:	Mortal enemies of fiat money.
Gold[1]:	Strips governments of ability to steal from citizens with inflation.
Gold[2]:	Enemy of fiscal insanity.

Golf:	Fairway excavation.
Good breeding:	Consists of concealing how much we think of ourselves and how little we think of others. (Mark Twain)
Good judgment:	Comes from experience - just like bad judgment. (Will Rogers)
Good old days:	When silver in a dime was worth more than a dollar today.
Good scare:	Worth more than good advice. (Proverb)
Good taste:	Enemy of humor. (?)
Gossip:	Social sewage. (George Meredith)
Govern:	"Rule" - by executive orders.
Government:	"Stop and Shop for every special interest in the country." (Jerry Brown, former governor of California.)
Government contract:	Return On Bribery – aka Rob.
Government math:	9%+4% = 3% unemployment.
Government stats:	Thundering inexactitudes.
Government work:	Where hard things take forever and easy things take even longer." (~ Richard D. Blodgett)
Graduation:	Onset of actual education.

	Caleb Spalding Atwood

Graduation present: Student loan invoice.

Grave: Place where the dead are laid to await coming of the medical student. (Bierce)

Guillotine: French cure for dissent.

Gun control laws: Reason for skyrocketing gun sales.

Gun laws: Protection for gangs, gangsters and politicians.

Hallucinations: Privacy, free speech, Bureau of Labor Statistics.

Hangover: Reward for life of a party.

Happiness: "Good health and a bad memory." (Ingrid Bergman)

Harry Reid: Democrat who contends that the US income tax is voluntary.

Hate speech: Any remark deep state elites and their toadies find offensive. (aka truth).

Head: Protrusion from body with which people think they think. (?)

Heartless: Cardiac donor.

Hell[1]:   "No other invention came as easily to man." (?)

Hell[2]:   Too good a place for warmongers.

“He’s a good man”:   Reason 19 prisoners gave for braking out of their cells to help a guard having a heart attack. (True)

“Hello”:   Foreplay.

Hurricane Harvey: Turned houses in Houston into swimming pools. (Guess how I know.)

“Interesting”:   Polite term for “idiotic.”

“It’s not mine.”   What Adam told Eve and politicians have been telling voters ever since.

“Me and him”:   Testament to quality of education throughout much of America.

“So am I”:   Obama’s response when Chicago Mayor Rohm Emanuel said he was in love with him?

“Verbicide”   “Words used so often and indiscriminately that they have lost their cutting edge.” (?)

Hero: Cornered coward.

Higher prices: Cure for high prices. (?)

Hillary[1]:   Deep state candidate.

Hillary[2]:   Hear no Benghazi, speak no Benghazi, remember no Benghazi, Clinton.

Hillary’s victories: Getting Obama and Trump elected.

     Caleb Spalding Atwood

History[1]:   An account, mostly false, of events, mostly unimportant, brought about by rulers, mostly knaves, and soldiers, mostly fools. (Bierce)

Hoffa: Taken out because he posed a threat to mobsters' piggy bank?

History[2]:   The sum of biased biographies. (~Thomas Carlyle)

Homeland Security: Organization charged with protecting politicians from citizens.

Honest Politician: "One who when bought, stays bought." (Political boss Simon Cameron)

Honesty[1]:   "Trait that pleases some and astonishes others." (Alexander Pope)

Honesty[2]:   Keeps almost as many people out of prison as campaign contributions. (?)

Honesty[3]:   Last resort.

Honesty[4]:   "Incompatible with amassing large fortune." (Mohandas Gandhi)

Honesty[5]:   "Not an issue in politics, it's a miracle." (Will Rogers)

Houston Astros: Hold major league record for one-game winning streaks.

Houston Rocket fan: Cautiously pessimistic.

HSCs: High Speed Computers that can steal millions almost as fast as governments can steal billions.

Humans: "Only creatures able to behave irrationally in the name of reason." (NY Times, September 30, 1975)

Humor: Truth. (Victor Borga)

Hush money: Bankster bonuses.

Ice sickle: Global warming logo.

Idea: Brain sprinkle, storm, tsunami, wash?

Ideal creditor: "Someone with faith, hope, charity and Alzheimer's." (?)

Ideal guest: One who stays home. (~ Edgar Watson Howe)

Immunity: License to squeal.

Impartial: Unable to perceive personal advantage. (~ Bierce)

Incarcerated: Temporarily unelectable.

Income tax returns: "World's most imaginative fiction." (Herman Wouk)

Income tax: "Makes more liars out of Americans than golf." (Will Rogers)

Incompetence: "Something you can always count on

  Caleb Spalding Atwood

	from politicians and bureaucrats." (Jim Roberts)
Incumbents:	Politicians who fool 51% of voters 100% of the time.
Independent:	Progressive, conservative or carnal mystic under protective cover.
Inedible:	Diet friendly.
Infinite idiocy:	Warmongering.
Infinite:	"Only two things are infinite, the universe and human stupidity - and I'm not sure about the latter." (Albert Einstein)
Infinity:	Projected near term national debt.
Inflation pays:	Zimbabwe 100 trillion dollar bills, once worthless, are now selling for up to $60 as souvenirs.
Inflation too low:	Money not becoming worthless fast enough to suit the Fed.
Inflation[1]:	Either mild or wild depending upon whether you believe government statistics or your bank balance.
Inflation[2]:	Lifeblood of the Federal Reserve.
Inflation[3]:	Too low - unless you're addicted to eating.

Inflation[4]:   "Means governments use to confiscate citizens' wealth." (?)

Inheritance: Dead giveaway.

Innocent: Undetected.

Insider trading: Crime for citizens, perk for congress.

Insufferable: Politicians, contrarians, spouses or siblings - when they are right.

Insufficient Inflation: Cost of food, clothing, housing and transportation

not rising fast enough to satisfy the Fed.

Internet[1]:   Enemy of governments and liberal media.

Internet[2]:   Where you can buy a nickel's worth of something worthless on sale for only a dollar.

Intrepid: Clueless.

Investors: Sheep waiting for shearing with ultra-high-speed stock trading computers.

Invisible   Bureau of Labor Standards characterization of people whose benefits have run out.

Irrefutable: Witness-free.

IRS[1]:   Internal Retribution Service.

             Caleb Spalding Atwood

| IRS[2]: | So short-handed they barely have time to harass conservatives. |

IRS[2]: So short-handed they barely have time to harass conservatives.

ISIS: Profit center for Military-Industrial Complex.

It's not mine: What Adam told Eve - and politicians have been telling voters ever since.

Jail: Adult education.

Japan: Forced to outsource American jobs to China.

Jealousy[1]: "Tribute meritocracy pays to genius." (Bishop Fulton J. Sheen)

Jealousy[2]: "Something you have to earn." (Arnold Schwarzenegger)

Jeb: Son of a son of a Bush.

JFK retort: "I'm sure it was unanimous." (President Kennedy's response when told republicans passed a resolution criticizing him).

Jobs: America's primary export.

Jockey Shorts: Best seat in the House. (Actual Ad)

John F. Kennedy: Enemy of Deep State Jonathon Gruber pilloried for saying "Americans are stupid" when most in congress proved it by voting for the Affordable Care Act without reading it.

July 4th:   Pyromaniac play day.

Justice: When bankers guilty of massive theft face penalties nearly as severe as citizens get for J-Walking.

Kaddafi death knell?:   Selling oil for gold rather than U.S. dollars.

Kleptomaniac: "Man who helps himself because he can't help himself." (Henry Morgan)

Larry Ellison: President of Oracle paid himself $1 last year, raising concern that he might double it this year and set a precedent for other executives to double their pay.

Laryngitis: Cure for verbosity.

Laughter[1]:   Cheap medicine. (Lord Byron)

Laughter[2]:   "The shortest distance between two people." (Victor Borge)

Laws: Obstacles that yield to cash.

Lawyer: One skilled in circumvention of the law. (Bierce)

Libel: Is it libelous to refer to someone as a donkey's derriere without naming them - when everyone knows exactly who you are talking about?

Lie[1]:   "The greater the lie, the greater the

                     Caleb Spalding Atwood

chance it will be believed." (Adolph Hitler)

Lie[2]: Thundering inexactitude. (?)

Lie[3]: Tortured truth.

Lie[4]: aka campaign promise.

Lies: "Go halfway around the world before truth can put its pants on." (Churchill)

Lightning: Nickname for slowpokes.

Loafing: Power resting.

Long live death: 20th century Spartan war cry - "Viva la Muerte."

Loquacious: Politicians who act as if they get paid by the word. (~ Bob Dole)

Lottery[1]: Tax on people who are not good at math. (Bierce)

Lottery[2]: Winning is like going to heaven without the inconvenience of dying.

Love[1]: Temporary insanity curable by marriage. (Bierce)

Love[2]: "A woman may fall out of love with her husband, but he won't." (Zsa Zsa Gabor)

Love[3]: Heart attract.

Low calorie: Low taste.

Lucky: Losing politicians.

Lucrative: "Contributions" to Clinton "Charitable" Foundation.

Lugubrious: Succinct in DC.

Machiavelli: Vilified for describing things as they were rather than as they should have been. (?)

Mainstream Media: Dedicated to ousting president Trump - in a non-partisan way, of course.

Mainstream media: Liberal lapdog.

Man[1]:   Domestic animal susceptible to training. (?)

Man[2]:   The only animal that blushes - or needs to. (Mark Twain)

Managing: Getting paid for home runs others hit. (Casey Stengel, former NY Yankee manager)

Margaret Thatcher: "Plutonium blonde." (Arthur Scargill)

Marijuana tax: Competitive advantage for illegal pot pushers.

Marijuana[1]:   Medicine for people who aren't sick - yet.

Marijuana[2]:   Dopiate of the people.

 Caleb Spalding Atwood

Marriage license: Declaration of dependence.

Marriage[1]:   The state or condition of community consisting of a master, a mistress and two slaves, making in all, two. (Bierce)

Marriage[2]:   Triumph of infatuation over finance.

Marriage[3]:   "Institution that destroys relationships." (Gloria Steinem)

Marriage[4]:   Only war in which people sleep with the enemy? (?)

Marriage[5]:   Triumph of sex over common sense.

Martyr: Man who allows his wife to cook, clean house and shop without complaining.

Martyrdom: "Only way to become famous without ability." (Schopenhauer)

Masochists: People who plead guilty for the thrill of being abused.

Medical Marijuana: What's next - medical Martinis, Mai Tais, Manhattans?

Meet: "Encounter" in congress.

Menacing: Truthful.

Mental Kleptos: "People who bundle off truths and later, by virtue of the fact that they have been stored in their brain cells, consider them to be their own." (Classic examples - "Bucky Fuller's" Dy-maxion House and Geodesic Dome.)

Michelle's legacy:	Students smuggling lunch into schools.
Middle class:	Anyone with at least a minimum wage job.
Middle East:	Product testing ground for Military-Industrial complex.
Military Complex:	Making a killing, killing.
Millionaires:	People who create products in US, manufacture them in China and sell them at Wal-Mart.
Millions:	Fines politically connected may have to pay for stealing billions.
Mind:	Not a prolific gut to be stuffed with knowledge. (?)
Minimum wage:	Ample for people who don't like to eat, drink, drive or sleep indoors.
Miniskirt:	Floor length after taxes.
Mischievous:	Daughter or Mr. and Mrs. Chievous. (Groan!)
Misfortune:	Easy to bear - in others. (Proverb)
Misremember:	Lie.
Mob money:	Brute finance.

     Caleb Spalding Atwood

Molotov: Russian's favorite cocktail.

Money[1]:   Root of all politics.

Money[2]:   Not an object, an idol.

Monogamist: Man who only harasses one woman at a time.

Moonshine: Last untaxed beverage.

Moses: Nickname for person with a sub-zero IQ.

Murderer: "One guilty until proven insane." (~Clarence Darrow)

Myth: Strong US dollar.

National debt: "Blessed are the young, for they shall inherit it." (Herbert Hoover)

National emergency: When politicians cannot get paid.

National Security[1]: Rationale for starting wars to further enrich the filthy rich.

National Security[2]: Pretense for ignoring constitutional rights.

National Security[3]: "False flag." (Ron Paul)

Natural Disasters: Hurricanes, tsunamis, floods, earthquakes, politics.

Necessities: Water, oxygen, whiskey. (Bill Bonner)

Needed: Peace Mongers.

Negative interest: Fee depositors pay for the privilege of loaning money to banks.

Negotiate: Capitulate in D.C.

Next President: Candidate who vows to rescind the most executive orders.

Nikita Khrushchev: "Politicians are all the same. They promise to build a bridge when there is no river."

No kidding: Birth control. (Groan)

No money down: Booby trap.

Noise: Political discourse.

Nonpartisan: Happy, no matter which party loses.

Normal: Lacking imagination. (Jean Dubuffet)

Notarize: Attest to misstatement.

Notorious: Successful.

NRA: Steadfast opponent of personal cannon possession - in crowds.

NSA[1]: American Gestapo.

NSA[2]: Hades gift to privacy.

NSA[3]: "Protecting" US by making enemies of former friends.

 Caleb Spalding Atwood

Nude:	Debriefed.
Nymphomania:	A terrible thing to waste.
Oath of office[1]:	I solemnly swear not to discriminate based upon race, creed, color, age, sex or stupidity.
Oath of office[2]:	Prevaricratic oath.
Obama:	Would have lost if unopposed. (~Mort Sahl)
Obama Epitaph:	"All the wars I started were republicans' fault."
Obamacare:	In fairness, president Obama did manage to boil his healthcare law down into a mere eleven million, eight hundred and eighty-five thousand words.
Obediocrasy:	Nirvana for rulers.
Ocean:	A body of water occupying about two-thirds of a world made for man - who has no gills. (Bierce)
Odd odds[1]:	Odds of Nancy Pelosi eloping with Rush Limbaugh.
Odd odds[2]:	Odds of politicians celebrating - with truth serum.
Old age[1]:	"Once you're over the hill you begin to pick up speed." (Schopenhauer)

Old age[2]:   Superannuated adolescence.

Old age[3]:   When hair grows faster in noses than on noggins.

Old age[4]:   When you can't even remember what you meant to forget.

On welfare: Gainfully unemployed.

Open borders[1]:   Must be maintained so terrorists and thieves aren't accidently prevented from entering US.

Open borders[2]:   Nirvana for criminals, gilded invitation for ISIS.

Open windows: Exits for distraught bankers.

Opponent: Muddy-minded.

Opposition: Party that prevents it's opponent from running amuck - by hamstringing it. (~Bierce)

Optimism[1]:   Hoping what you know ain't so.

Optimism[2]:   Pessimism after happy hour.

Optimistic: Delusional.

Optimists: People who are rarely right (as opposed to pessimists who are rarely wrong).

Options: If you don't like your lawyer you can

Caleb Spalding Atwood

change your lawyer. If you don't like a law, you can change your mind.

Oratorical:	Sleep-inducing.
Originality:	"Undetected plagiarism." (Ralph Inge)
Outlaw:	Perpetuate.
Oxymoronic:	The trouble with president Obama was that you could not believe a word he said, whereas the trouble with president Trump is that you can.
Party of Peace:	The most inane claim you'll hear if you live forever and a year.
Pass:	Fail to flunk.
Patriot Act:	aka US constitution nullification Act.
Patriotism:	The willingness to kill and be killed for trivial reasons. (George Bernard Shaw)
Peace keeping:	Sacrificing American soldiers to prevent enemies from killing each other.
Peace Mongers:	What the world needs now, always has - and always will.
Peace treaty:	Intermission.
Peace[1]:	Calm before the norm.
Peace[2]:	Enemy - of Military-Industrial complex.

Peace[3]:	A period of cheating between two periods of fighting. (Bierce)
Peace[4]:	Interval between wars for enemy identification - or creation. (?)
Peace[5]:	Job killer.
Penny saved:	Congressional oversight. (Hal Lee Luyah)
Personality:	People don't have to be beautiful, to be beautiful - or vice versa.
Pervert:	Gay guy who also likes women.
Pessimism:	"Mark of superior intelligence." (John Kenneth Galbraith)
Pessimist:	Someone who is rarely wrong.
Pessimists:	Men who think all women are bad (as opposed to optimists who hope they are). (?)
Philosophy:	A route of many roads leading from nowhere to nothing. (Bierce)
Pick-up line:	Will you marry me?
Pink ink:	Not red, but risky.
Plagiarism:	Academic kleptomania.
Plasma:	aka Bloody Mary.
Plea:	"If you have a complaint, send it to me

	in writing - on the back of a check." (~Earl Stanley Gardner)
Plutocracy:	Government by the rich, for the rich, and newly elected - who will soon be rich.
Poet:	Artist who paints pictures with words.
Political advantage:	Fear that opponent would be even worse.
Political discourse:	Putting mouth where money is - or vice versa.
Political malady:	Selective deafness.
Political Promises:	Diaper overloads.
Political speech:	Americans will defend to the death politicians' right to make fools of themselves.
Politically correct:	BULLverized.
Politician[1]:	"Person trained in the art of inexactitude." (Edward R. Murrow)
Politician[2]:	Man who stands for things he thinks others will fall for. (?)
Politicians[1]:	Speak as if they're paid by the word. (Bob Dole)
Politicians[2]:	Experts at providing indecipherable answers to unequivocal questions.

Politicians[3]:	Devil's disciples.
Politicians[4]:	Blame throwers.
Politicians[5]:	Bankster lapdogs.
Politics[1]:	Slithers in where common sense fears to tread.
Politics[2]:	Cure for prosperity.
Politics[3]:	The conduct of public affairs for private advantage. (Bierce)
Politics[4]:	Derived from "poly" meaning "many" and "tics"- small blood-sucking insects. (Chris Clayton)
Politics[5]:	Sure cure for insomnia – and prosperity.
Poll numbers:	Reverse Trump's and he'd be a very popular president.
Pollution solution:	Bottled air.
Ponzi:	Patron Saint of Federal Reserve.
Popular:	Promiscuous.
Popularity:	Reward for making miserable people feel good about themselves.
Population control:	Over 50 million abortions since Roe v. Wade.
Pot fanatics:	Don't mind if it maims brains since they're not using theirs.

     Caleb Spalding Atwood

Potty seatbelt:	OSHA requirement?
Pray:	"Don't pray for the president, pray for the country." (Edward Everett Hale)
Prayer[1]:	Oh Lord, if there is a lord, save my soul, if I have a soul. (Ernest Redaj)
Prayer[2]:	Dying atheist's last resort.
Predictable:	Deceased.
Premeditated:	Poorly planned.
Preposterous:	"Crock' in common parlance.
Presidency:	If Hillary is ever elected, will Chelsea be far-left behind?
President Obama[1]:	Greatest gun salesman in the history of history.
President Obama[2]:	Soul mate of Saudi who said "I am a prince so I can do whatever I want."
President Reagan:	"Awaken me any time of national emergency, even if I'm in a cabinet meeting."
President[1]:	Warmonger in chief.
President[2]:	Anyone who aspires to be president should be disqualified on that basis alone.
Prevarication:	Damage control in DC.

Prevaricationary   Dictionary of political terms.

Printing press: Life blood of Federal Reserve.

Privacy[1]:   Extinct, with creation of the million square foot Spy Center in Utah recording everything we write, sing or say.

Privacy[2]:   You remember privacy, don't you Methuselah?

Privacy[3]:   Fond memory.

Pro: Undetected con.

Procrastination: "The art of keeping up with yesterday." (Don Marquis)

Profane: Bleepish.

Profanity: Tolerable when hitting thumb with hammer - or paying taxes.

Public Relations: If five executives get mega million bonuses, ten get one thousand and thousands get none, report executive average.

Puerto Pobre: *nee* Puerto Rico.

Pulitzer Prize Lie: "Under my plan no family making less than $250,000 a year will see any form of tax increase." (President Obama re: Obamacare.)

Punctuality: Thief of time. (Oscar Wilde)

    Caleb Spalding Atwood

Putin:	Demonized for doing what US is doing.
QE to infinity:	Must have Keynesians dancing in their graves.
QE^1:	Makes Ponzi seem like a piker.
QE^2:	Inflate gate.
Quarterback:	Tax refund.
Quid pro Quos:	Blacks give democrats unwavering support. Democrats give blacks open borders.
Quips^1:	Best way to belittle.
Quips^2:	Make you want to tear your clothes off and dance in aisles - unless you're ashamed of your body. (~ Kingston Trio)
Quotation:	The act of repeating erroneously the words of another. (Bierce)
R & D:	"Rip off and duplicate." (Andy Hunt)
Radical^1:	"Person with both feet planted firmly in the air." (President F.D. Roosevelt)
Radical^2:	Conservative in California.
Radicals:	Democrats, according to Republicans and vice versa.
Ramshackle:	Affordable.

Rape: Offense octogenarians plead guilty to for the honor of being accused.

Rare: Politician more concerned with being right than getting reelected.

Rare prayer: "Lord help me - help others."

Reality: "Something to rise above." (Liza Minnelli)

Recession: Raging since 2008.– mainstream media propaganda notwithstanding.

Recollect: To recall, with additions, something not previously known. (Bierce)

Recreate: Plagiarize.

Redd Foxx roast: "We will march forward to a better tomorrow as soon as groups like blacks, negroes and colored can resolve their differences." (Steve Allen to a black audience.)

Regulate: Manipulate.

Reliable: Never failing to fail.

Repartee: Something we think of 12 hours too late. (Twain)

Republicrat: Nonpartisan.

Reputations: "90% of politicians give the others a bad reputation." (Henry Kissinger)

Research: Efforts to confirm preconceived assumptions.

Retaliation: Refusal to export vodka and borscht to Russia.

Retreat: Attack to the rear.

Retribution: China hacking us - for hacking them when we found out they were hacking us - for hacking them.

Reverse engineer: Polite term for purloin.

Revolution[1]:   Abrupt change in the form of misgovernment. (Bierce)

Revolution[2]:   When people have had enough of not having enough.

Ridicule: World's most potent weapon.

Riots: When people are no longer willing to suffer in silence.

Risk: If you never risk anything you may be risking even more. (?)

Robots: Fantastic for profits - disasters for unemployed.

Ron Paul: Bright light in political dungeon.

Rulers: "Beneficiaries of men who do not think." (Adolph Hitler)

Rush hour: "When nothing moves."
(Robin Williams)

Sacrifice: Doing without what others don't have.

Saddam's crime: Selling oil for Euros, rather than US dollars.

Sage advice: Never hire a man with calluses on his derriere.

Saint: Dead sinner, revised and edited. (Bierce)

Same: Odds of winning lottery whether you play or not. (Dorothy Parker)

Sanity: Curable by marriage.

Savings accounts: Bankster piggy banks.

Schizophrenia: Cure for loneliness.

Screwed: What Americans got for the $1.7 trillion in bullion Obama paid for an agreement Iran refused to sign, will not, and has not enforced.

Second marriage: Triumph of hope over experience. (Samuel Johnson)

Seconds: Projected incumbency and life span of judges who rule against NSA spying.

Secrecy: Blame in hiding.

Secret police:	Gestapo in Hitler's time, NSC in ours.
Secrets:	Three can keep them, if two are away. (John Heywood)
Secure:	Incarcerated.
Self -confidence:	Faith in a fool. (~ Edgar Alan Poe)
Self-love:	"Beginning of a life-long romance." (Oscar Wilde)
Self-pity:	What woman - black, white, brown, yellow, pink or polka-dot, would feel sorry for herself if she were rich and could have had toys like Air Force One? (Hillary?)
Senate:	Inane asylum.
Senator Rockefeller:	Unique because he was rich *before* he got elected.
Senior citizen:	Superannuated adolescent.
Sentences for pols:	Hard labor in liquor stores.
Serial prevaricators:	Politicians.
Shaking hands:	Sex after 70.
Shotgun wedding:	"Wife or death." (Houston Chronicle cartoon)
Shout!:	When in doubt.
Sign at my gym:	"If you're too weak to re-rack weights

you use, please ask one of the girls at the desk for help."

Skeleton: Diet company role model.

Slavery[1]: Government without the consent of the governed. (Jonathon Swift)

Slavery[2]: Should not have been opposed because it was the law of the land.

Snoring: Synonym for boring.

Snowden: Vilified for endangering dishonesty.

SOB: Son Of a Bachelor?

Socialism: Fair and equitable distribution of poverty.

Sodium pentothal: Desperately needed in D.C.

Sodomy: Tailgating.

Solar energy: Perpetual pollution solution.

Soldiers: Hired killers. (Jim Karger)

SOS: Save our socialism?

Spam: Conflicting opinion.

Spanking: Physical education.

Speech: Free due to excessive supply.

Speechless: Under oath.

Spike Jones:	Godfather of musical mayhem, who would have made Beethoven wish he was deaf. (?)
Starvation:	Cure for dieting.
Stonewall:	Nickname for former Attorney General Holder.
Student loan invoice:	Graduation present.
Student Loans:	Taken over by government to protect banks from losing money on profitable investments..
Stupid acts:	Lame-brainers.
Stupidious:	Stupid *and* hideous.
Stupidislation:	Raising taxes to promote prosperity.
Subconscious:	Key to creativity that is usually unemployed.
Success[1]:	Making enough money to meet obligations you wouldn't have if you did not make so much money. (?)
Success[2]:	Being right half as often as the weatherman is wrong.
Success[3]:	Unpardonable sin against our fellows. (Bierce)
Suicide:	Severest self-criticism.

Surgeon: Organ grinder.

Surprise[1]:   Princeton University professor con-
                          cludes US is no longer a democracy.
                          (April 2014)

Surprise[2]:   Do criminals in government that
                          Snowden exposed expect him to be
                          prosecuted for it?

Surreal: Conservative in Hollywood.

Syria: Where CIA armed militia fought FBI
                          armed militants. (True)

Tact: "The ability to describe others as they
                          see themselves." (Abe Lincoln)

Taste: Enemy of creativity. (Pablo Picasso)

Tattoos: Unemployment assurance. (~ Bill Cosby)

Tax audit: Reward for contributing to party out
                          of power.

Tax: Fee for all.

Taxes[1]:   Tribute enabling government by the
                          rich and for the rich, to further enrich
                          the rich.

Taxes[2]:   Walletectomies. (James Napoli)

Taxidermists: Differs from tax collectors in that they
                          leave a hide. (~ *NY Times*, February
                          1963)

                        Caleb Spalding Atwood

Ted Cruz:	Senator whose citizenship would not have been questioned if he'd been born in Kenya.
Temporary sanity:	Explanation when a politician says something sensible.
Tenure:	Reward for prolonged incompetence.
Term limits:	Because politicians, like diapers, regularly need changing.
Terrible trade:	Five violent enemies for one American deserter.
Terrorist toys:	Drones.
The Fed[1]	Winning war against fiscal sanity.
The Fed[2]:	Satan's gift to the ultra-rich.
Thief's prayer:	Lord help me - help myself.
Theft:	Negative interest rates.
Thinking:	OK if not habit-forming.
Thunder sprinkle:	Monsoon in California.
Toast:	Wishful drinking.
Tolerance:	Forgiving those not quite as guilty as ourselves.
Traitor:	Sobriquet for anyone exposing duplicity, in DC.

Trans-Pacific Trade:	"First time in history victors sued for peace and vanquished called for unconditional surrender, and got it." (~ Abba Eban)
Trigamy:	Two mates too many.
Trophy husband:	Apparition. (~ Woman's' Lib)
Trophy wife:	Wealthy widow.
Trump[1]:	Criticized for scaring hell out of people, but who needs hell in them?
Trump[2]:	Making a far better president than Hillary - but so would Mr. Michael Mouse.
Trump political advantage 1:	He wasn't Hillary.
Trump advantage 2:	All Hillary's voters were alive.
Trust me:	Preposterous plea in DC.
Truth serum:	Banned in DC.
Truth[1]:	Felony in D.C. (ask Snowden).
Truth[2]:	Stranger than fiction. (Mark Twain)
Truth[3]:	"The greatest enemy of the state." - (Joseph Goebbels, Nazi Minister of propaganda)
Truth[4]:	Not an excuse - in politics.

 Caleb Spalding Atwood

TSA: If not for TSA some people wouldn't
                        have any sex life at all.

TSA agent: Dream job for armature proctologist.

Two-faced: Flexible.

Ultimate praise: "Fabulous job of picking parents."

Ultimatum: Last demand before concession.
                        (Bierce)

Under oath: Reason witness keeps calling plaintiff
                        a liar.

Unemployed: Congress - whatever it is doing is *not*
                        working.

Unemployment[1]:   Flip side of automation.

Unemployment[2]:   Not all bad because it's not necessary
                        to cheat on taxes.

Unions: Enemies of employers who treat em-
                        ployees like enemies.

US Constitution: Fond Memory.

US dollar: As good as all the gold theoretically
                        stored in Fort Knox.

US Foreign policy: Enough to make a laughing hyena cry.

US Press: Citizen watchdog turned oligarch lap-
                        dog.

USA Constitution: Political inconvenience.

Vote: "The instrument and symbol of a free-man's power to make a fool of himself - and a wreck of his country." (Bierce)

Voter ID: Scheme to deprive illegal aliens of the right to vote illegally.

W.C. Fields: Spent a lot of time searching the Bible for loopholes.

War[1]:   God's way of teaching geography. (Bierce)

War[2]:   Successor to cannibalism for population control.

Warmongers: Devil's disciples.

Weaker sex: Intimacy after 60.

Wedding: A ceremony in which two persons undertake to become one, one undertakes to become nothing, and nothing undertakes to become supportable. (Bierce)

Wedding present: Lifetime supply of sex. (aka Nirvana.)

Wit: Educated insolence. (Aristotle)

Women: God's second mistake. (Nietzsche)

Words: Weapons.

Writing: Recreational torture - like golf.

       Caleb Spalding Atwood

Zero: Difference between Democrats and Republicans. (Drudge)

2020 Election: "None of the above" should win in a landslide.

CHAPTER II

MILLIONS IN MINUTES

Altogether there are 765 quips in the first chapter. In Appendix A there are pegs, including strange animals like:

> assassin bug, jumbo octopus, fairy penguin, fanged water deer, fried-egg jellyfish, frog-nosed hawk, hellbender salmon, ice-cream cone worm, pink-fairy armadillo, poodle bird, poodle moth, punk rock bird, square lip rhino, star-nosed mole, umbrella bird.

These can be coupled with an enormous number of things animals (human aberrations excepted) do not need to create tens of thousands of alliterative quips. In Appendix B there are pegs and pivots that can be employed to create thousands of these that rhyme.

Ms. Steinem's quip can be formulated as A needs B like X needs Y, with "A needs B" as its *premise*, and "X needs Y" as its *contrast*. Hereafter, X's will usually be referred to as "pegs" and Y's as "pivots." Example: A woman needs a man (peg) like a flamingo needs a firecracker, fiddle orFerrari (pivot).

Why not continue to use animals as pegs and objects as pivots? Good question. Glad I asked. It's because individuals, organizations, companies, and virtually any other entities can often be substituted for "fish" or "bicycle" in Ms. Steinem's quip. More on this later, but for now, let's take a further look at how her quip can be adapted to create an enormous number of other quips.

With human aberrations excepted, an animal's needs are basic-water, oxygen, food, safety, sex and suitable environments. Many may devour Twinkies, Tootsie Rolls, lollypops or crepe suzettes, if given the opportunity, but they do not *need* them. Consequently, incongruity is a lock to surface when contending that animals, human aberrations excepted, cannot live without anything but basics. Accordingly, there are a gigantic number of things that can be substituted for "bicycle" in Ms. Steinem's quip.

All of this raises a burning question, namely, with so many alternatives, how do we decide which to use? The best options will usually be among those featuring alliteration, rhyme or both because they make things we write, read, sing or say sound better and tend to make stronger and more lasting impressions. As Clement Wood, author of the *Complete Rhyming Dictionary* put it, "Alliteration and rhyme work because they are pleasing to the ear and our inner sense of music and are readily retained in our minds."

To illustrate, wouldn't numerous other pivots starting with an "f", including thirty that follow, have sounded at least as good as a woman needs a man like a fish needs a:

> face lift, fair, fedora, Ferrari, Ferris wheel, fiddle, fifth, filibuster, filleting knife, firecracker, fish, flak jacket, flamethrower, flask, flintlock, flugelhorn, flute, fly rod, flyswatter, football, fork, formaldehyde, fox hole, freezer, Frisbee, frying pan, fudge, furnace or furrier?

     Caleb Spalding Atwood

Incidentally, Steinem's quip equates women with fish and that is not too swift - even for a man with a food taster.

Apropos of little, perhaps, but alliteration and rhyme have something in common few are likely to realize. While alliteration is usually repetition of similar sounds at the beginning of lines whereas rhyme is usually the repetition of similar sounds at the end of lines. Together

Alliteration and rhyme are the music of language.

They are not essential, but they usually make what we write, sing, shout or say sound better, make stronger impressions, and stick. Poe's Raven, Lincoln's Gettysburg Address and the Star Spangled Banner are classic examples. Excerpts:

The Raven

The Raven published in 1845, is likely one of the most memorable of all English poems. However, at the risk of making Edgar Allen Poe groan in his grave, stripped of rhyme and alliteration, it is likely that the *Raven* would forever and ever more have amounted to little more than a famously forgettable rant by a poet perturbed by what he believed to be a bird:

> Once upon a midnight dreary, while I pondered, weak and weary, over many a quaint and curious volume of forgotten lore. While I nodded, nearly napping, suddenly there came a tapping. As if someone gently rapping, rapping at my chamber door. "Tis some visitor,"

I muttered' taping at my chamber door - Only this and nothing more.

Alliteration: weak ... weary / quaint ... curious / upon ... ponder

Rhyme: dreary ... weary / door ... more ... lore ... / napping ... tapping ... rapping ...

Gettysburg Address

"Four score and seven years ago our forefathers brought forth upon this continent, a new nation, conceived in liberty, and dedicated to the proposition that all men are created equal. We cannot dedicate, We cannot consecrate-we cannot hallow this ground. The brave men, living and dead, who struggled here have consecrated it, far above our poor power to add or detract. The world will little note, nor long remember what we say here ... government of the people, by the people, and for the people, shall not perish from the earth."

Alliteration: cannot ... cannot ... cannot / dead ... devotion ... died / dedicated ... dedicated fathers ... forth ... freedom ... new nation ... note ... nor poor ... power ... people ... people ... people...perish / say here... did here ... little ... long

Rhyme: four … score / dedicated … created … conse-
                crated

The Star Spangled Banner

Oh, say, can you see? By the dawn's early light

What so proudly we hail'd at the twilight's last gleaming;

Whose broad stripes and bright stars, thro' the perilous fight,

o'er the ramparts we watch'd were so gallantly streaming.

And the rocket's red glare, the bombs bursting in air.

Gave proof through the night that our flag was still there…

Oh, say, does that star-spangled banner yet wave

o'er the land of the free and the home of the brave!"

Alliteration: early … light … fight / broad … bright /
                bombs … bursting…/ rockets' … red / star …
                spangled

Rhyme: gleaming … streaming / wave … brave / air
                … there / early … proudly / light … twilight
                … fight / glare … air

Precarious Premises

Ms. Steinem's premise worked because it was startling at the time,
but her contrast - "a fish needs a Ferarri" - had a drawback. Using
animals in quips usually works, but in her case using "fish" laid a

hard-broiled egg because contrasting women with fish, is ill advised - even for the aforementioned people with food tasters.

Incalculable numbers of quips

The previously mentioned incalculable number of ways to express opinions must have sounded borderline bizarre, so let's take a look at it. There are 705 animals (pegs) and 925 things none of them need (pivots) juxtaposed alphabetically in Appendix A (pp.?). These alone are sufficient to create 652,125 alliterative quips and this is easy to increase enormously considering that there are estimated to be 9.7 million species of animals extant, including at least dozens recognizable enough to be used as pegs or pivots if for most audiences. There are also an almost incalculable number of things animals do not need - like languages, toys, approximately 100,000 diseases, billions of publications tools, games, sports, hobbies, clothes, cosmetics, mathematics, natural disasters, professions, etc. Let's not forget the aforementioned 68 verbs in Appendix C that can usually be substituted for "need" and skyrocket quip volume.

Incidentally, creating alliterate quips is easy with help from Appendix A that contains lists of animals (pegs) juxtaposed alphabetically against things they don't need (pivots). Examples:

Pegs

Baboons, badgers, bagpipes, barracudas, barn owls, basset hounds, bats, beagles, bears, bass, beavers, Bengal tigers, bunnies, burrows, butterflies, etc.

Pivots

Badminton, baccarat, babushkas, bagpipes, ballet, bands, bandwagons, banjos, banks, bars, barbers, barrettes, barges, baseballs, bugles, bullets, etc.

Women need men like baboons, badgers, barnacles, etc. need, cherish, adore, etc., badminton, baccarat, banjos or dozens of other things (nouns) whose names start with "b."

Appendix B (pp. ??) facilitates creating quips that rhyme by listing pegs adjacent to pivots that rhyme with them. Example:

> Fox: ballot box, bobby socks, boom box, boondocks, Botox, chicken pox, dreadlock, flintlock, grandfather clock, idiot box, jack-in-the-box, jukebox, Maalox, mailbox, musk ox, ox, Pandora's box, pillbox, press box, safe deposit box, sandbox, shamrock, shot clocks, shuttlecock, skybox, smallpox, soapbox, squawk box, stock, strongbox, toolbox, Xerox

Does a fox really need bobby socks, smallpox, a jukebox, Xerox, etc.? Additionally, the 68 verbs previously mentioned among 125,000 in the English language will usually work well. Examples from Appendix C:

Accumulate, ache for, adore, amass, applaud, appreciate, believe in, care for, caress, cater to, cherish, cling to, coddle, collect, confide in, covet, crave, cuddle, delight, demand, depend upon, deserve, desire, dote on, dream of, embrace, esteem, exalt, fancy, fondle, guard, hail, haunt, hunger for, idolize, laud, learn, like, lionize, long for, love, miss, nurture, pamper, praise, prize, promote, protect, ravish, regale, relish, rely on, require, respect, yearn for, revel in, revere, savor, seek, stockpile, swear by, thrill, treasure, value, want, weep for, welcome, worship.

Women adore, etc.
Trump like liberals adore, etc.
Limbaugh

In this format, men and women at odds with one another - Clinton and Trump, Divorcees, etc. can be substituted for Limbaugh along with virtually any company, organization, or other entity can be substituted for an individual - GM needs Honda, CBS needs NBC, politicians need Truth serum, and so on. Actually, it's easy to increase the number of quips by adding additional pegs or pivots. If, in the unlikely event you cannot think of any, or if you want to see if you can find better alternatives, all you need do is refer to Appendix A (pp. ?) where you will find lists of animals (pegs) juxtaposed alphabetically against things they do not need (pivots). Then, in Appendix B you'll find dozens of pegs juxtaposed next to lists of things they do not need that rhyme with them.

Ms. Steinem's quip can be formulated as A needs B like X needs Y- in which "A needs B" is its *premise*, and "X needs Y" is its *contrast*. (Hereafter, X's will usually be referred to as "pegs" and Y's as "pivots." Why not continue to use "animals" as pegs and "objects" as pivots? Good question. Glad I asked. because individuals, groups, organizations, companies, or virtually any other entities can be substituted for "fish" or "bicycle" in her quip. More on this later, but for now, let's explore how her quip can be adapted to create a gigantic number of other quips.

With human aberrations excepted, animal needs are basic-water, oxygen, food, safety, sex, companionships and suitable environments. They may devour Twinkies, Tootsie rolls, lollypops, popsicles, crepe suzettes, etc. if given the chance, but they do not *need* them. Consequently, incongruity is a lock to surface when contending that animals need (i.e., cannot live without) anything but the aforementioned basics. To illustrate, an enormous number of things (pivots) can be substituted for "bicycle" in this quip. My favorite? A Woman needs a man like a fish needs a Ferrari.

Alliteration and rhyme work because they "are pleasing to the ear and readily retained in our minds." (~Clement Wood, author of the *Complete Rhyming Dictionary*). Apropos of little perhaps, but alliteration and rhyme have something in common, namely that alliteration is repetition of similar sounds at the beginning of lines, whereas rhyme is repetition of similar sounds at the end of lines.

CHAPTER III

ADJECTIVE BASED ALLITERATIVE QUIPS

It is easy to create quips with adjectives. Simply contrast them alliteratively with opposites of what is expected of them. Following are examples derived from Appendix A.

As gaudy, giddy, goofy, greedy, etc. as a

> gander, gar, garter snake, gator, gazelle, gecko, gerbil, giraffe, gnu, goat, goldfinch, goldfish, goose, gopher, gorilla, grackle, grasshopper, Great Dane, greyhound, grizzly bear, groundhog, grouper, grouse, guide dog, guinea pig, guppy

As pretty, popular, proud, etc. as a polka dot:

> packrat, palomino, panda, panther, parakeet, parrot, partridge, peacock, pelican, penguin, perch, peregrine, pheasant, pickerel, pig, pigeon, piglet, pike, pinto, piranha, pit bull, polecat, polliwog, pony, poodle, porcupine, porpoise, possum, potbellied pig, prairie dog, prawn, pronghorn, puff adder, puffin, pug, pullet, puppy, puma, python

As sexy, scintillating, spellbinding, etc. as a

> sailfish, saluki, sandpiper, sapsucker, sardine, scallop, schnauzer, schnook, scorpion, scrod, seagull, sea hawk, seahorse, seal, shark, Sheltie, shrimp, sidewinder, silkworm, skunk, skylark, sloth, snail, snake, snipe, sow, spearfish, spider, springbok, squid, squirrel, stag, stallion, starfish, starling, steelhead, steenbok, stink bug, stingray, stork, sunfish, swallow, swan, swordfish.

It is easy to create hundreds more. Examples:

As agile as:

> A doctor operating on a malpractice attorney.
> flies with one working wing.
> jellyfish jockeys.
> kangaroos on pogo sticks.

As attractive as:

> bouquets of used sneakers. (P.J. O'Rourke)
> a moose in a papoose.
> the body of a 27 year old - taxi. (?)
> the south end of a horse going north. (Coleman Brown)

As common as

> 400 pound diet-book authors.
> abortion clinics with 2 year waiting lists.
> being arrested for public sobriety
> hunting in zoos.
> moonshine for breakfast.
> learning to drive by accident?

Maalox on tap
pace cars at snail races.
parachutes that open on contact.
pigs in penthouses.
selling cows to buy milk. (Peter D. Schiff)
sloths arrested for speeding .
wake-up calls at Forest Lawn. (Joey Adams)
whitewalls on manure spreaders.
shutting a mouth with a foot in it.

As dumb as

asking a woman where she got her facelift.
     (P. J. O'Rourke)
marrying a self-made widow.
selling sheep to buy wool.
telling a woman she's younger than she looks.
     (P.J. O'Rourke)
water-proofing diapers

As easy as

finding gold in ghettos
finding needles in hay stacks
giving centipedes pedicures.
juggling jellyfish
selling silicone at beauty contests

As enjoyable as

enduring adversity-in others. (Mark Twain)
the first week of a first marriage
giving others the benefit of your inexperience

herding kittens with a cattle prod
shutting a mouth with both feet in it

As effective as:

breaking a leg to beat the draft
circular firing squads
shaving with a power saw
sterilizing storks to control population growth.
wake-up calls at Forrest Lawn (Joey Adams)

As happy as:

vultures in blood banks
pet tarantulas
pickpockets in nudist colonies
vegans with hunting licenses

As normal as:

broad waists and narrow minds
deficits in D.C.
gaining weight on a diet
second skydiving accidents

As rare as:

hypochondriacs who are actually sick
polka dot diapers
reform school scholarships
teachers playing hooky

As popular as:

doctors who keep stethoscopes in freezers (?)
kids who know how to play bagpipes - but don't. (?)

night ping-pong (spectator sport I invented using phos-
     phorous paint.)
pythons in petting zoos

Many other adjectives also work. As:

crooked as a barrel of snakes (Byron King)
crucial as pace cars at snail races
crude as asking a woman with 10 kids what her hobby is.
dangerous as someone with nothing to lose (Goethe)
devout as a praying mantis
difficult as eating éclairs. (~Theodore Roosevelt)
exciting as dress poker.
happy as a hypochondriac who is actually sick
happy as a pig in popcorn.
implacable as an ex-wife suing for alimony
     (Wm. Wycharly)

CHAPTER IV

RIPS

Rips in our context are sharp comments, retorts, responses or re-marks that often lurk on the outer limits of lunacy. Examples:

- If they'd say that out in the country, it would really help the crops. (?)

- Corporations do not create jobs, government does.

- Inflation is dangerously low.

- Millions of jobs were created while president. Obama was in office (reportedly

Many, if not most, were temporary, contractual or part-time without benefits.)

- The US dollar is as good as gold. (Apologies to gold.)

- We need to pass a law to find out what is in it. (?)

- Trump will defend to the death a Democrat's right to make a fool of himself - and democrats will be happy to return his "compliment."

My favorite response to comments like these was by retired Democratic Senator Zell Miller who said

"If they'd say that out in the country, it would really help the crops."

In the examples that follow, "X" represents whomever or whatever you deem worthy of a particular accolade

- Can X possibly be as young as he acts?

- Each of X's speeches is better than his next one.

- How much would it matter if X lost the rest of his mind?

- If X is a trophy husband, his wife is a terrible shot.

- If X is at wits end, he didn't have far to travel. (Lord Byron)

- If X is not lying, he's taking obscene liberties with the truth.

- If X really loved his wife he would never have married her.

- If X wasn't married, he'd be his own worst enemy.

- If X's breath could be liquefied it would get 20 mpg - in a tank.

- Occasionally X comes dangerously close to making sense.

- Only a pig considers X an equal. (Winston Churchill)

          Caleb Spalding Atwood

- Only half the lies X tells are premeditated.

- People don't know what they would do without X, but would love to find out.

- People wouldn't believe X if he swore he was lying.

- The baby looked like X – until it was turned right-side up. (?)

- The only problem with (president) Polk is that he drank too much water." (~Sam Houston)

- The world is X's jail. (~John Donne)

- There aren't enough diapers in DC to absorb X's campaign promises.

- There is always the haunting possibility that X is telling the truth.

- Truth flies south when X opens his mouth.

- With X it is monkey see, donkey do.

- X is a lock to make the Prevaricators Hall of Fame.

- X buys things he doesn't need to impress people he doesn't like.

- X can be miserable at times - daytimes, night times, spring times…

- X can compress the most words into the smallest idea of any man I ever met. (Abraham Lincoln)

- X can lick his weight in wild flowers. (W.C. Fields)

- X can say less with more words than a politician.

- X can't be wrong all the time, but it's not for lack of effort.

- X can't decide whether or not he's undecided.

- X cannot leave "bad enough" alone.

- X could sell designer diapers in a zoo.

- X couldn't even make a hyena laugh.

- X couldn't pass a drug test if he studied for it. (?)

- X doesn't have much to be modest about. (Winston Churchill)

- X doesn't stretch truth - she hangs it.

- X finds it more convenient to let his hair grow than to wash his neck. (?)

- X fired his secretary for a mistake she wouldn't make. (?)

- X graduated magna cum loaded.

- X has a pornographic memory.

- X has bacon, eggs and hangovers for breakfast. (?)

- X has been unreliable since he was in diapers.

- X has found the cure for popularity.

- X has high friends in low places.

     Caleb Spalding Atwood

- X has lied and taken bribes, but not since yesterday, so it's time to move on.

- X has more of the virtues people dislike and none of the vices they admire. (Winston Churchill)

- X has no redeeming ignorance.

- X has overcome the odds against failing.

- X has the backbone of a chocolate éclair. (Theodore Roosevelt)

- X hasn't a single redeeming defect. (Disraeli)

- X is a brother without the "r."

- X is a devout atheist.

- X is a pants-wetting coward. (Ann Coulter)

- X is a perfect person to NO!

- X is a recovering teetotaler.

- X is a squander maniac. (Winston Churchill)

- X is a superannuated infant.

- X is always eager to make up your mind.

- X is an honorary member of the alcohol of fame.

- X is as brave as a pregnant pole-vaulter.

- X is at the age where he can't take "yes" for an answer.

◆ X is crazy about Y - if you omit "about Y."

◆ X is doing his best to make Right-to-Lifers change their minds.

◆ X is his own favorite charity.

◆ X is inebriated with the exuberance of his own verbosity. (Disraeli)

◆ X is intermittently honest.

◆ X is like a cock who thinks the sun rises to hear him crow. (Georg Eliot)

◆ X is madly in love with her husband's wife.

◆ X is not as much under the affluence of inkahol as some thinkle may peep. (Eleanor K. Lehman)

◆ X is outspoken by no one. (Jack Parr)

◆ X is predictably unpredictable.

◆ X is so brave he'd wrestle a lion wearing pork chop underwear - if he could find one. (Alonzo Brown)

◆ X is so contrary he'd oppose a Catholic becoming Pope. (~Ann Coulter)

◆ X is so meticulous he only brushes one tooth at a time.

◆ X is so morose obituaries cheer him up.

◆ X is so persuasive he could convince Sumo Wrestlers to join Weight Watchers.

 Caleb Spalding Atwood

- ✦ X's ignorance is encyclopedic. (Abba Eban)

- ✦ X's mind is only fertile in the agricultural sense.

- ✦ X's mother told him if people at a party started swearing he should pick up his pants and come home.

- ✦ X is so poor he can't even afford a Democrat.

- ✦ X is so sick he looks like the picture on his driving license.

- ✦ X is so skinny she could hula hoop a fruit loop. (Katie Austin)

- ✦ X is the devil in disguise.

- ✦ X is tired of being a virgin, but who wouldn't be at sixty?

- ✦ X is too lazy to loaf.

- ✦ X isn't as strong as he smells.

- ✦ X isn't nearly as young as she acts.

- ✦ X isn't sure he's agnostic.

- ✦ X isn't young enough to know everything. (Oscar Wilde)

- ✦ X knows everything about nothing.

- ✦ X never fails to fail.

- ✦ X never hurts anyone's feelings - unintentionally. (Oliver Hertford)

- ✦ X never uses a tack hammer when a sledgehammer will do.

- X occasionally stumbles over the truth, but quickly picks himself up. (Churchill)

- X only hits babies in self-defense. (?)

- X only tells the truth when it's easier than memorizing. (~ Charles Krauthammer)

- X relishes in his self-applause. (Cato)

- X sings by ear through his nose.

- X suffers from a lack of laryngitis.

- X thinks the Jones' are trying to keep up with him.

- X was popular, even before she became a virgin.

- X went on a diet and lost 5 pounds - before brushing his teeth.

- X would be rich if egomania could be monetized.

- X wouldn't have graduated from kindergarten if he hadn't been dating his teacher.

- X: A serial prevaricator.

- X: Conclusive proof that God has a sense of humor.

- X: has taken the cure for honesty.

- X: platinum bald.

- X: A one trick phony.

- X: Is as happy as a pig in a python.

    Caleb Spalding Atwood

- X: Such a good saleswoman she could sell designer diapers in a dime store.

- X's thrilled from the tip of his toes to the top of his toupee.

- X's blind date turned out to be his ex-wife. (?)

- X's face looks like a bouquet of sore elbows. (Phyllis Diller)

- X is too lazy to loaf.

- X can never find enough to complain about – but it's not from lack of effort.

CHAPTER V

PROVOCATIVE QUESTIONS

We usually ask questions to get information, but **asking questions can also be an interesting and effective way to express opinions.** Following are dozens you can use as is, or adapt to express your own opinions. Among them are questions styled after comedians like Hillary Clinton, Phyllis Diller, Bob Hope, Joe Biden, and deceased pro football player Ron Kramer, Let's start with him.

After an intramural water polo game between our fraternities at the University of Michigan, the Sigma Chi's invited Sig Eps to their fraternity house for a few beers. During the evening, people kept drifting away until only yours truly and Ron Kramer, an All American football player at Michigan and All Pro subsequently with the Green Bay Packers, remained. During our conversation, he told me how one of his fraternity brothers had awakened him late at night before a Michigan–Ohio State football game, screaming "Ron, Ron, I've come to beat Ohio State!" Ron realized that his brother needed help and followed in hot pursuit as he fled down four flights of stairs and onto State Street, a main drag at U of M. During this, Ron came up with a great provocative question – for himself. "I'm chasing this guy down State street in the middle of the night in my underwear and I'm going to try and convince people he's the one who is crazy?" Onward…

Banks

- How many bankers avoid prosecution because they know too much - or too many?

- How many bankers should be wearing black-and white-striped suits?

- Is it a bigger crime to rob a bank - or to open one? (Ted Allen)

- Is it legal for Goldman Sachs to sell tons of paper gold to drop its price and then accumulate more of it than any other entity in the world?

- What is or was the life expectancy, if he still has one, of the pundit who coined the term "International Bank Crime Cartel"?

- Where will convicted banksters, if there ever are any, serve time - yachts, country clubs, penthouses?

Blacks

- Isn't the National Basketball Association conclusive proof that all men are not created equal?

- How long would borders have remained open if, prior to

     Caleb Spalding Atwood

mid-terms, blacks had vowed not to vote unless president Obama closed them?

◆ Wouldn't it have been ironic if president Obama had motivated blacks to vote for Trump?

◆ If, as former attorney general Eric Holder maintained, opposition to Obama is racist, are blacks also oppose NSA, Fast & Furious, tax increases or wars, racists?

Executive Compensation

◆ How many CEOs would quit if their compensation was limited to a mere million bucks a year?

◆ How high would the minimum wage go if executive pay was limited to 20 times what lowest employees are paid - as GM founder Alfred P. Sloan once mandated?

◆ How loud would executives scream if their pay could only be increased if all employees' pay increased proportionately?

Federal Reserve

◆ Is the Fed trying to make the great depression in the 1930s seem like the "good old days?"

◆ In September of 2015, the Fed said, "Lower inflation is a drag on worker income," but how can being able to afford necessities like food, medicine, gas, clothing, etc. for less, be a "drag" on income?

- Wouldn't it be wonderful if citizens, like banks, could buy municipal bonds from the Fed at two percent interest and purchase tax-free municipal bonds that pay up to 3.50% with their proceeds?

- Is it realistic to expect the Fed to make decisions favorable to average citizens when it is owned, controlled and run by big banks and the oligarchs who own them?

- With gold and silver excepted, is there any currency in the western world that is backed by more than the full faith and credit of the bankrupt country issuing it?

- Was Zimbabwe the Federal Reserve's role model – or vice versa?

- How long will it be before US and Canadian dollars, Euros, Pesos, Yuan and other un-backed paper currencies, become collector's items like Zimbabwe's 100 Trillion dollar bank notes that are now selling for up to $60 each as souvenirs?

Freedom

- In Saul Alinsky's *How to Create a Social State,* a book he dedicated to Lucifer, what were the the eight levels of control that must be obtained to create a social (i.e., socialist) state.

- Healthcare: Control healthcare and you control the people.

- Poverty: Increase the poverty level as high as possible, poor people are easier to control and will not fight back if you are providing everything for them to live.

　Caleb Spalding Atwood

- ◆ Debt: Increase the debt to an unsustainable level. That way you are able to increase taxes, and produce more poverty.

- ◆ Gun Control: Remove the ability of citizens to defend themselves from the Government. That way you are able to create a police state.

- ◆ Welfare: Take control of every aspect of lives - Food, Clothing, Housing, and Income..

- ◆ Education: Take control of what people read and listen to – take control of what children learn in school.

- ◆ Religion: Remove the belief in the God from the Government and schools.

- ◆ Class Warfare: Divide the people into the wealthy and the poor. This will cause more discontent and it will be easier to take (tax) the wealthy with the support of the poor.

How would you, revered reader, currently rate the US on each of those just mentioned?

Gold

- ◆ Is the U.S. dollar "as good as gold" when the 262 million ounces of gold our government claims to have, but refuses to verify, would have to sell for over $250,000 per ounce to back our $20 trillion in US national debt, including $171 trillion in unfunded liabilities as of August 2016), and undoubtedly trillions more by now?

- How many US citizens realize that our national debt averaged over $400,000 for each and every one of us in January of 2017 and several dollars more subsequently.

- Does the U S have any of the gold it claims to have, but will not verify?

- Can anyone be happier about the U.S. manipulating the price of gold than those in China, India, and Russia, in particular, who are amassing it at bargain prices – in some cases to eventually issue a gold-backed currency?

- Are the Chinese amassing gold (and lately silver) to back the Yuan so they can supplant the U.S. dollar as the world's primary reserve currency?

- Would investors and governments dislike gold and silver if, like US dollars, they could be created with their own keystrokes?

- Who is right, Warren Buffett who disparages gold - or his congressman father who disagreed with him because, as he put it, "A gold standard prevents governments from confiscating citizens' wealth with inflation"?

- Do people who denigrate gold because "you can't eat it", eat fiat?

- Was the former budget director, Dr. Paul Craig Roberts, who ought to know, correct when he said, "All the U.S. gold is gone?"

- If gold is a "barbarous relic" as many of its critics maintain, are the Chinese, Russians, Indians, Europeans, Americans, and others collecting it, barbarians?

 Caleb Spalding Atwood

- Are the Chinese amassing gold to back the Yen as the world's foremost international currency?

- Is gold eventually going to replace the US dollar as the world's reserve currency - as Jim Rickards, noted financial analyst and editor of *Strategic Excellence*, predicts?

- Are any other US markets manipulated as extensively as the gold and silver markets?

- Does the US have any of the 142.7 millions of ounces of gold it claims to have, when a former U.S. Treasury Secretary said it was all gone decades ago?

Guns

- Can anyone blame politicians who voted for Obamacare for wanting to disarm citizens?

- Are police being militarized to protect or control citizens?

- How low would the Chicago murder rate go if killers killed by other killers were not counted?

- Was the massive amount of ammunition purchased for firemen so they can shoot out fires?

- If the Supreme Court rules against citizens owning guns, wouldn't that be tantamount to ruling that citizens cannot rely on any constitutional protection whatsoever - or has that already been established?

- Will stricter gun laws prevent the suicides that account for half of gun deaths in the US? (per the Houston Chronicle, December 17, 2015)

- Do politicians want to confiscate guns to protect citizens - or themselves?

- Won't new guns that can shoot around corners make wars seem like hunting in zoos?

- How many major gun opponents live in safe neighborhoods and have guns, bodyguards, or both to protect themselves?

- How many of the thousands of people killed by guns had guns to protect themselves?

- What percent of people killed by guns were murderous or murderous gang members?

- Do people who oppose hunting think that the animals they eat – cattle, pigs, chickens, etc.- die natural deaths?

- What's next, hunting ducks with slingshots?

- Which former US president said: **"The rifle and pistol are equally indispensable...the very atmosphere of firearms everywhere restrains evil interference - they deserve a place of honor with all that is good."** (Clue: He used to sleep with a woman named Martha.)

Illegal Drugs

- Should cocaine maiming brains be an issue, when people using it are not using theirs?

- If pot is illegal because it is addictive and mind-numbing, why isn't alcohol?

- Are states legalizing marijuana for health reasons or to get in on the action?

Inflation

- Would former Fed chairwoman Yellen have claimed that inflation was too low if she had done her own shopping?

- Who is right. The US government when it claims our deficit is $20 trillion, or Boston University professor Laurence Kotlikoff, who maintained it was actually $211 trillion early in 2017?

- How strong would the "strong" U.S. dollar be if it weren't measured against collapsing currencies in countries as bankrupt as, or even more bankrupt, than the U.S.?

- What money has the most inherent value: Euros, Pesos, Rubles, Swiss Francs, US Dollars, Chinese Yuan or U.S. nickels? (Clue: Save your nickels.)

- How long can the U.S. treasury continue to borrow $1.43 for every dollar of tax revenue received? (As per James Dale Davidson, September 2016.)

- Has Obamacare enabled doctors, hospitals and drug companies to raise prices as much as the government takeover of student loans has enabled universities and textbook publishers to skyrocket tuition and textbook prices?

◆ If you're old enough to remember fiscal sanity, then did you happen to know Alexander Hamilton?

IRS

◆ Is the IRS as "impartial" as the NSA?

◆ Would anyone object to Warren Buffet paying higher taxes voluntarily to ease his conscience about being under-taxed?

◆ How can citizens trust the IRS when, on September 30, 2013, over 1,300 IRS employees who were delinquent in paying their own taxes received bonuses?

◆ How often does the IRS scare the "o" out of "hello"?

◆ Should pay and-benefit costs of illegal aliens be tax deductible business expenses at times when millions of Americans are unemployed, underemployed, or on welfare?

Jobs

◆ What would be the impact on the Bureau of Labor Standards' unemployment calculations, if college graduates in kindergarten drop-out jobs were not counted as fully employed?

◆ How much does actual unemployment in the U.S. vary from reported unemployment?

- How many million Americans have lost full time jobs or had their hours, pay, or benefits cut during our "recovery?"

- How long will it be before unemployment offices are run by robots?

- Why is the U.S. paying billions in welfare to citizens when our cities, roads, schools, bridges, etc., desperately need work that many, if not most of them, are either capable of doing or quickly learning to do?

- How long will it be before robots start creating other robots to displace employees?

- What would the reaction be if the Bureau of Labor Standards reported under- employment as well as employment?

- When calculating unemployment, does the US government count grade-school dropouts the same as graduate engineers?

- Will 30-hour work-weeks become common or compulsory in another decade or two, when nearly half of existing manufacturing jobs are expected to be automated, if not outsourced to other countries?

- If 66% of Americans lost their jobs, would the Bureau of Labor Statistics report U S unemployment as 4.9 or 5.1%?

- What will happen to employment when robots combined with computers can do, or train most workers to do nearly any job - in any language -almost anywhere in the world?

- How long will it be before robots start building robots?

Markets

- Why did it take so long before Wal-Mart was forced to stop having suppliers put "Made in America" tags on products made elsewhere?

- How many investors realize brokers keep stocks they buy for them in their firm's name so they can rent them to investors, who lower their prices by selling them short?

- How low would the Dow go if not for periodic fiat infusions by the Fed?

Media

- Isn't it refreshing in America to know if you say or do something stupid enough, you are likely to get your name in the papers and possibly even appear on TV?

- Is internet "neutrality" a scheme to turn the internet into a public futility?

- If Gallup asked a hundred citizens whether Democrats or Republicans were the most honest, and one said Republicans and two said Democrats, would lock step mainstream liberal media report "Only half of Americans believe Republicans are honest?"

- Wouldn't it be enlightening if the media were to publish a list of donors to politicians who vote for highly controversial laws?

- Would Moses have a prayer of getting the Ten Commandments through Congress today?

◆ If Fox News is as "fair, balanced and unafraid", as it so often claims, why hasn't it exposed the massive manipulation in the gold and silver markets?

Obama Care

◆ If president Obama's Affordable Care Act is so wonderful, then why did congress exempt itself?

◆ When the U.S. Supreme Court approved the Affordable Care Act, did it realize it was forcing millions of citizens to purchase coverage they do not need and frequently cannot even use - like maternity benefits for singles, and seniors?

◆ Will Bill Clinton's calling the Affordable Care Act, the "craziest thing in the world" make any difference whatsoever to Democrats?

◆ If politicians had known then what they know now, would they have voted for the Affordable Care Act? (Apropos of nothing perhaps, but in October of 2013, I e-mailed this question to 39 of the democratic Senators who voted for Obamacare and got two answers. Both were unresponsive, but one did say it was nice to hear from a fellow North Carolinian. (I am a Texan.) I also e-mailed it to Fox News, where Chris Wallace asked it of retired Democratic Senator Joe Lieberman, who said "Yes.")

Politics

◆ Did Americans vote for Trump because they thought he was the only candidate who could save them from Democrats *and* Republicans?

◆ Democrats in the Senate are furious with Republicans because they won't confirm presidential appointments. Republicans are furious with Democrats because they won't bring up bills passed by the House. Who is to blame Democrats, Republicans, or those of us who voted for them?

◆ Did Trump win or did Hillary lose?

◆ Did some Democrats oppose Obama Trade because they knew they'd be under intense Affordable Care-like pressure to pass whatever Obama negotiated - no matter how pitiful? (Voila! "Free Trade" Agreement.)

◆ Do "coyotes" smuggling people into the U.S. make political contributions - or does it just seem as if they must?

◆ If lies and duplicity were contagious, would Washington be quarantined?

◆ Is there anything in Washington as definite as deficits, bribes (aka campaign contributions) and taxes?

◆ Have there ever been politicians in the U.S. who have not become far wealthier while in office?

◆ How can Republicans claim to be fiscal conservatives when U.S. national debt increased $1.8 trillion under President Reagan, $1.554 trillion under president H.W. Bush, and $5.8 trillion under President G.W. Bush?

          Caleb Spalding Atwood

◆ How long will citizens be forced to forfeit the last vestiges of privacy and freedom in the guise of "national security"?

◆ How many cities have more registered than eligible voters?

◆ How many US presidents should have gone to jail?

◆ How long would campaign speeches last if candidates were required to take truth serum before giving them?

◆ How long would Obama have left our borders open if illegals had been likely to vote for Republicans?

◆ How many more dead people voted for Hillary than Trump?

◆ How many large political "contributions" are not written off as business expenses?

◆ How much would Hillary's multi millions in speaking fees eventually have cost U.S. taxpayers if she had been elected?

◆ If con is the opposite of pro, is **con**gress the opposite of **pro**gress? (*Houston Chronicle*. 5/31/16)

◆ If Obama had a choice between eliminating all ISIS warriors or all Republicans, how long would it have taken him to decide?

◆ If there'd been Pulitzer Prizes for soliciting illegal campaign contributions, how many politicians would have won them?

◆ If politicians were paid what they are actually worth, wouldn't it often be in violation of minimum wage laws?

◆ In a world teeming with atheists, isn't it refreshing to know all politicians believe in something - even if it's just campaign contributions?

◆ Isn't applauding Obamacare because some of it works kind of like applauding Al Capone because he only killed some cops?

◆ Is Snowden endangering democracy with facts?

◆ What did Hillary do when Secretary of State beside send thousands upon thousands of e-mails?

◆ Why shouldn't Oprah Winfrey, who expressed interest, have run for President when she was at least as unqualified as anyone else who was running?

◆ How many Americans would've voted for Attila the Hun if he'd been running in 2016?

◆ Will Democrats or Republicans ever admit they are anti-austerity parties, like the party in Spain that goes by that exact name?

◆ Will there ever be an honest US election when it takes millions to elect representatives, and billions to elect presidents?

◆ Would Americans be better off if congress took even more time off?

◆ Wouldn't it be refreshing if Americans had incentives to vote *for*, more often than *against*, politicians?

◆ If president Trump were to nominate Abe Lincoln incarnate to the U.S. Supreme Court, would any Democrats vote for him?

◆ Isn't the grave danger of running for mayor of Chicago the possibility that you might get elected?

◆ If Ivan the Terrible had been a Democrat, would mainstream media have called him Ivan the Terrific?

    Caleb Spalding Atwood

◆ Would Obama have become president if not for "voters" no longer plagued with having to breathe?

◆ Was Sadaam murdered because of weapons of mass destruction that did not exist or because he refused to cede control of Iraqi oil to the oligarchs?

◆ What politician knows ten ways to make love but can't get a date - yet upon hearing he'd never been refused, pleaded guilty for the honor of being accused?

◆ If lies, bribery and duplicity were contagious, would congress be quarantined?

Privacy

◆ What provision of the U.S. Constitution gives a president the right to usurp the Constitution and rule unilaterally with executive orders?

◆ Does the "G" in G-mail stand for "cc: Government"?

◆ Was mainstream media's aggressive opposition to Donald Trump a detriment or asset for him in the 2016 election?

◆ Was the problem with President Obama that it was hard to believe anything he said - whereas the problem with president Trump is that it is not?

◆ Did people support Trump because they thought he'd be a better president than Benghazaillery or because they thought he wouldn't be as bad?

◆ How many voters oppose warmongers for president because they do not want to spend eternity looking up at the world from the bottoms of coffins?

◆ How viable would Hillary's bid for president have been be if she had not been married, if you want to call it that, to Bill?

◆ Were most voters *for* Trump - or *against* Hillary?

Rulers of the World (aka Deep State)

◆ Is North Korea or the international banking cartel an American citizen's most formidable enemy?

◆ How much illegal immigration would there be if the deep state suffered, rather than profited from it?

◆ Would oligarchs who rule the western world change, even slightly if they had to spend a year at the bottom, rather than top of the prosperity chain?

War

◆ How can citizens expect peace when war is the lifeblood of the massive military-industrial complex and source of their political campaign contributions?

◆ How much of the staggering U.S. debt, has been spent on wars to protect and preserve the U.S. dollar as the world's foremost reserve currency?

◆ Does the U.S. keep troops in 140 countries (per Ron Paul) to protect them and foster friendship - or to maintain control?

- Does the U.S. really need war for domestic political reasons, as former budget director Paul Craig Roberts once maintained?

- How many families did wounded warriors leave fatherless before they themselves were wounded?

- How much of the weaponry being used to kill U.S. soldiers was made by American-owned or controlled companies in the U.S. or elsewhere?

- How many terrorists, spies, saboteurs, thieves and other criminals get through our unprotected borders each day and why don't democrats want to stop them?

- What did the U S get from billions spent for wars in Iraq and Afghanistan, other than 7,845 dead U.S. soldiers?

- Should president Trump be castigated for being unwilling to wage a war against Russia that would likely have killed over a million Russians and as many Americans?

- Does a country "win" a war if it leaves more families fatherless, motherless, homeless and destitute than it's enemy?

- Miscellaneous

- If the Noble Peace Prize Committee could do two things over again, what shuld the second one be?

- Has any charity benefitted even remotely as much from the Clinton "Charitable" Foundation as the Clintons themselves?

- Did the Clinton Charitable Foundation have a price list?

- What's the life expectancy of the US$ as the world's reserve currency when China, Russia and other countries soon begin to trade with Special Drawing Rights?

- What is worse, telling someone to go to hell… or Chicago?

- How long will it be before cash is banned in the U.S to eliminate our last vestige of privacy?

- How many people realize that diet soda makes us fat? (Dr. Amy Lee, Bariatric physician.)

- How many grade schoolers are passing math with Alexis?

- If cash is outlawed in the U.S., won't the IRS put tax accountants out of business by calculating taxes with the data that it collects directly from bank accounts?

- Does the fact that the Patriot Act (aka. the U. S. Constitution Nullification Act) passed in five working days after 9/11 - faster than Congress usually takes to raise its own pay - make one wonder if Congress knew something the rest of us did not?

- Are the Chinese doing anything to protect themselves that we wouldn't or haven't already done to protect ourselves?

- How many unions would oppose automation if robots paid dues? (Joke. I hope)

- How many more people would vote if given the option of voting for "none of the above?"

- Who wanted to brighten and enliven Trump's inauguration, get a few laughs and amuse the nation, by junking the ceremony's traditional motif and having the band play "Inhale to the chief"?

     Caleb Spalding Atwood

◆ Why shouldn't leopards have stripes, lions have brightly spotted manes, kittens be wild, wolverines tame, and politicians admit it when they are to blame?

◆ Who is right: Al Gore, who maintains that Co^2 will kill everyone if it's not reduced to zero or Patrick Moore, co-founder of Greenpeace, who said "Without Co^2 all plants, and therefore all humans would die?

◆ Was former US treasury secretary Paul Craig Roberts correct when in a January 21, 2014 interview he said: "The Affordable Care Act does not provide care. It's a way to loot the poorest people and steal whatever assets they have…The poorest who are supposed to be helped are herded into Medicaid where any property they have is subject to estate recovery."

◆ What is more profane - telling someone to go to hell or Chicago?

◆ Where do people in hell tell people to go?

CHAPTER VI

QUIP, RIP & PROVOCATIVE QUESTION TIPS

The internet is teeming with information about creativity. Most impressive is how Osho, a brilliant, enlightened and prolific mystic from India who wrote over 650 books, explained the process of creation.

> "The true creativity comes out of sitting silently. When you are so totally quiet that there is no thought, no wave in the ocean of your being, out of this silence comes a different kind of creativity."

Gertrude Stein echoed him with

> "It takes a lot of time to be a genius. You have to sit around so much, doing nothing, really doing nothing,"

So did prolific American author James Altucher:

> "You actually have to shut down your brain to come up with ideas."

In essence, what they are saying is that creativity originates in one's subconscious and is distracted, blocked or erased altogether by radio, TV, conversation or anything else we hear, see, feel or think. Consequently, we are most creative when lying down, relaxed and undistracted - with paper close at hand to record ideas before they escape from our subconscious.

You might try this by priming your mind with all you know about a problem you are trying to solve, goal you are trying to reach or quip you are trying to create and then relaxing completely with your eyes closed and wait for ideas to surface. They will often be fleeting, so keep writing materials handy to write down at least the crux of them before they escape. It's also wise to have a small flashlight handy for this at night. As crazy as this may seem, it worked pretty well for Thomas Edison. He didn't keep a bed in his laboratory and take naps intermittently during the day because he was tired - and no one ridiculed his creativity.

Prepare

Have you have ever heard something idiotic or bizarre in a meeting, but been unable to think of a suitable (i.e., profanity-free) response? If so you might want to also keep a few quips on hand to brighten and enliven your comments, responses or presentations.

Returning to earth, a good way to write effectively is to jot down the crux of whatever you have in mind and then search for rhyming or alliterative alternatives for words you have used. If, for example, you think George H.W. Bush is nutty for wearing gaudy socks to get attention, you could say so in so many words, but a search for alliterative alternatives turns up dozens of options

     Caleb Spalding Atwood

including shock socks, sick socks, silly socks, snazzy socks, sordid socks, splashy socks, spooky socks, squirrely socks and surreal socks - any of which is likely to attract far more attention.

CHAPTER VII

AUTHOR / SOURCES

Caleb Spalding Atwood

I have emerged from a 60 year career in labor and employee relations that included negotiating and administering labor agreements with one or more local unions of 19 different international unions. It included training hundreds of managers for companies, industry associations and universities like Texas A&M, the University of Nebraska, the University of Houston (where I was an adjunct faculty member) and my alma mater, the University of Michigan).

In 1994, I compiled *The Quality of Management In America* based upon a survey Dr. Lynn Evans and I conducted with 19,347 employees working for 97 US companies. Our work received publicity ranging from mention in business magazines, American and Hispanic wire services to newspapers, including the *Wall Street Journal*. The *Journal* that did not say much about or work, but it's hard to complain when our work was mentioned us on its front page.

My work has been cited in *Communications Briefings, Incentive Magazine, Executive Excellence Magazine, HR Briefing*, Wikipedia, the *AMA Management Handbook* and *American Productivity and Quality Center* publications.

Background: I came up with my first quip when I was eight. It was in an art class where I was working next to an incredibly beautiful blond. She decided my painting needed help and went to work on it. I returned the favor and an art war ensued that I obviously won because she got so flustered that she blurted out "When you get old you're probably going to marry someone mean and ugly." My first quip? "Is that a proposal?" (If it had been, I would have accepted.)

Now for some serious stuff I haven't previously mentioned to anyone. I was meeting with Teamster International VP, Bobby Holmes in his office, formerly Jimmy Hoffa's, in Detroit on July 30, 1975 when Hoffa was abducted and murdered. Holmes was one of the founders of the Teamsters and the one who had re-cruited Hoffa. As labor relations manager of the *Detroit News*, I had met with him before as he helped keep a lid on the loose can-non Teamster who represented *Detroit News* Teamsters directly, but on this occasion there were no problems whatsoever at issue. Holmes simply invited me to visit and we had a very pleasant con-versation about nothing in particular that lasted from about ten a.m. into the afternoon. **As I was leaving, Chucky O'Brien,**

Hoffa's stepson, was hurriedly heading to an office next to Holmes. He appeared extremely upset and he was shaking, seemingly uncontrollably.

When news of Hoffa's disappearance and presumed murder began exploding throughout the media, O'Brian was considered by many to have lured Hoffa to his death. Author Charles Brandt interviewed Frank Sheeran, a prime suspect, and reported:

Sheeran's story on June 2,2004 as reported in WikiAnsweres.com was "on the day Hoffa disappeared, **Chuckie O'Brien drove Hoffa, Sheeran and mobster Sal "Sally Bugs" Briguglio to a house in Detroit.** Hoffa and Sheeran went into The house and the other two men drove off…"Sheeran says he shot Hoffa twice behind the right ear as part of a mob hit to keep Hoffa from reclaiming power in the Teamsters." (June 2, 2004, Fox News) and depriving the mob control of the Teamster pension fund.

In 2001, "The FBI matched DNA from Hoffa's hair with a strand of hair found (in the back seat of a 1975 Mercury Marquis Brougham) driven by a longtime friend he had, in effect, if not officially adopted, Charles 'Chuckie' O'Brien, on July 30, 1975." Putting Hoffa in a back seat was unusual, and possibly a warning from O'Brien because Hoffa always rode in the right front seat when being driven. Some surmise that O'Brien sat Hoffa there to alert him of pending danger, and that seems quite possible.

Police and Hoffa's family had long believed O'Brien played a role in Hoffa's disappearance. If so, that may explain why O'Brien was so extremely upset when I saw him shortly after Hoffa was murdered. Years later it finally occurred to me that Holmes may have invited me to visit while Hoffa was being taken out so he would have had an alibi if suspected of being involved. It also occurred to me that I could have offered at least circumstantial evidence about O'Brien appearing so extremely upset shortly after his step-father's disappearance. Unfortunately neither occured to me until years later.

Background. As Labor Relations Manager at the *Detroit News*, I was responsible for negotiating and administering labor agreements with fourteen international unions. Thanks no doubt to Holmes, there were, with one very brief exception I'll get to in a moment, no strikes during my tenure - even though there had been consequtive strikes of one, three and nine months prior to my arrival – and the loose cannon Teamster representative I dealt with directly routinely threatened to strike.

As an aside, Holmes was so powerful I don't think any union would have dared strike the *Detroit News*, or anyone else in Detroit, without his approval if it would have put any teamsters out on strike. Fortunately, during my tenure, my relations with all unions at the News, except the printing pressmen on a single occasion, ranged from good to excellent so strikes were never a serious issue, regardless of Schade's continual threats. What follows is not relevant to Hoffa, but I think you might find it interesting so I'm going to detour to it momentarily.

Immediately upon my arrival at the *Detroit News*, the pressmen "greeted" me with a "Chapel Meeting." Chapel Meetings consisted of pressmen staying in their locker room until the company capitulated on whatever they were seeking. I was told that over the years there had been over a 100 of them. That seemed impossible so I suspected it was an enormous exaggeration, but there was a fairly hefty stack of chapel meeting reports in an office file, so it may not have been much of one. I did not have time to read any of them with the day's paper imperiled and was confident that I could quickly end the Pressmen's chapel meeting. There was no burning issue at the time, so I assume the pressmen just wanted to show me how tough they were. That was unnecessary because I already knew following consecutive company-wide strikes of one, three and nine months that probably got me hired.

The chapel meeting "honoring" me was easy to end. All it required was having the pressroom manager announce that the company was going to start firing one pressman every minute until it ended. Voila! Instant success, and there were no further chapel meetings while I was at the News or, as far as I know, subsequently.

The pressmen knew they could not all be fired at once, but apparently had not considered prospects of being fired one at a time. When they did, they immediately abandoned their strike and went to work. If that had not worked, there was another option that might have, as it had previously when UAW members walked out to "greet" me upon my arrival as labor relations manager at a previous employer. I simply told the strikers as they walked out that the company would start mailing their paychecks to their homes if they did not get back to work immediately. They did. Why? Because they worked a lot of overtime and many, perhaps most of their wives did not know how much they were getting paid, thereby enabling them to set aside cash for emergencies, like beer. Whatever, results were immediate and production was not impaired appreciably by teamsters or any other union then or thereafter while I was Labor Relations Manager.

It's fun to tell about successes, and I had many, but I also had one especially irritating failure that I explained in a June 8, 2015 letter I wrote, signed, sealed and stamped, but decided not to send to Michael Barone, the brilliant senior political analyst at the *Washington Observer*, with whom I had corresponded in the past. Following is the gist of what was in it. Early in September of 2014 I figured out how to get the border closed-quickly easily and legally. All it required was for black leaders to plead with blacks nation-wide to vow to withhold votes in the forthcoming hotly contested mid-term, if Obama did not immediately begin closing the border."

With the senate up for grabs, I was confident that the pressure on Obama would have been insurmountable, so I called and then e-mailed the idea to a black friend who was a law school professor, to see if he might help. He was sympathetic, but nervous about getting involved.

Soon after my e-mails to him were intercepted and my phone calls blocked. On one occasion I received a message saying his phone wasn't working, but efforts to reach him would continue. A week later, I received a message saying all my calls had been refused. That was obviously a lie because he and I had been close friends for over thirty years and soon after he called me. Unfortunately, our connection was so garbled I could not understand what he was saying so nothing came of that. Incidentally, I suspect that the garbled transmission may not have been accidental. A day or so later, I tried calling him again but failed. Meanwhile all my wife's and my incoming calls at home were blocked. At one point, she even got a busy signal when she tried to call our land line with our cell phone.

Soon after, I was kicked off G-mail altogether and lost all my e-mail address and about a hundred e-mails I had saved. When I tried to reconnect, I had to complete a form that, among other things, required me to report my cell phone number. I thought it was a ruse but complied and was reinstated. Two days later I was kicked off again. In order to get reinstated I had to provide a secondary e-mail address. I did, but was still not reinstated, but never had any of my saved messages returned.

Soon after, when endeavoring to sign up with Yahoo, I was informed that a review of my files had to be completed before I could be accepted. What files? I had not done any business whatsoever with Yahoo so there were none. I made a copy of Yahoo's notice and enlarged it so I could read some tiny light blue print apart from the rest of the text. That print gave me the option of bypassing the review so I did and, in fairness to Yahoo, I have been using it ever since without any difficulty whatsoever - although I would not be surprised if NSA still gets copies of everything I write on the internet. If so I pity them, but in sum, I'm afraid our right of privacy as America is but a fond memory.

NSA's job is presumably to protect Americans against terrorism, but blacks are not terrorists and these tactics were clearly to protect democrats who might have been in dire straits in the forthcoming midterms if not for blacks' usual solid support.

One last point. I've been working on this book for years without incident until a year or so again when my attempts to add to, edit or transmit it to anyone were blocked. I suspected that someone had planted a bug in my text to thwart it so I typed a fresh copy and have subsequently been able to print and transmit it freely. I can only conclude that some people definitely do not want this book to get published. So much for our presumed rights of privacy and free speech in America.

APPENDIX A

ALLITERATIVE PEG & PIVOT QUIP OPTIONS

A Pegs:
Abalone, Adder, Afghan, Airedale, Akita, Albacore, Albatross, Alligator, Alpaca, Amoeba, Anaconda, Anchovy, Angelfish, Angleworm, Ant, Anteater, Antelope, Ape, Appaloosa, Archerfish, Arctic Fox, Armadillo.

A Pivots:
Abacus, Accelerator, Accident, Accordion, Accountant, Acne, Acrobat, Aerobics, Aids, Airbag, Aircraft, Airmail, Airplane, Airport, Air rifle, AK47, Alarm clock, Alcohol, Algebra, Alibi, Alimony, Allowance, Almanac, Alphabet, Altimeter, Ambassador, Ambulance, Ambush, Ammunition, Amnesia, Amtrak, Annuity, Anorexia, Antifreeze, Anvil

B Pegs:
Baboon, Badger, Bald Eagle, Baltimore Oriole, Bantam Rooster, Barnacle, Barn Owl, Barracuda, Bass, Basset hound, Bat, Beagle, Bear, Beaver, Bedbug, Bee, Beetle, Beluga, Bengal Tiger, Billy goat, Bighorn, Bird, Birddog, Bunny, Burro, Butterfly, Barnacle, Barn

Owl, Barracuda, Bass, Bat eared fox, Bengal Tiger, Basset Hound, Bat, Beagle, Bear, Beaver, Bedbug, Bee, Beetle, Bighorn, Billy Goat, Bird, Bison, Black Bird, Bird of Paradise, Black Drum, Black Lab, Black Mamba, Black Vulture, Bloodhound, Blowfly, Bluebird, Bluefish, Bluegill, Blue Jay, Blue Racer, Blue Shark, Blue Whale, Boa, Boar, Bobcat, Boll Weevil, Bonefish, Bonito, Booby Bird, Border Collie, Boston Terrier, Boxer, Box Turtle, Brittany Spaniel, Bronco, Brook Trout, Buck, Buffalo, Bug, Bull, Bulldog, Bullfrog, Bull Moose, Bull Shark, Bumblebee, Bunny, Burro, Bushmaster, Butterfly, Buzzard.

B Pivots:

Boutonniere, Bowling Ball, Bowtie, Brassier, Brass Band, Brail, Branding iron, Brassier, Break Dance, Breeches, Briefcase, Bronchitis, Broom, Bubble Bath, Bubblegum, Buckshot, Bugle, Buick, Bulldozer, Bullhorn, Bumper Car, Bungee Jump, Bunny Slippers, Burlesque, Bursitis, Bustle, Butcher, Buzz saw.

C pegs:

Calf, Calico Cat, Canadian Goose, Camel, Canary, Capybara, Cardinal, Caribou, Carp, Carrier pigeon, Cat, Caterpillar, Catfish, Centipede, Chameleon, Chamois, Cheetah, Cheshire Cat, Cheetah, Chick, Chickadee, Chicken, Chihuahua, Chimpanzee, Chinchilla, Chipmunk, Chowchow, Cicada, Clam,

     Caleb Spalding Atwood

Clownfish, Clydesdale, Cobra, Cockatiel, Cockatoo, Cockroach, Cod, Coho, Collie, Colt, Condor, Coon, Copperhead, Coral Shake, Cormorant, Condor, Cottonmouth, Cottontail, Cougar, Cow, Cowpony, Cowbird, Coyote, Crab, Crane, Crappie, Crawdad, Crawfish, Cricket, Croc, Crow, Cub, Cuckoo, Cutthroat trout, Cuttlefish.

C Pivots: Cab, Cabaret, Cable, Caboose, Caddie, Cadillac, Café, Cage, Calculator, Calendar, Calisthenics, Calliope, Calypso, Camcorder, Camera, Cancer, Candelabra, Cannon, Canoe, Canteen, Cappuccino, Carbine, Carnival, Carousel, Carpool, Cartridge, Cash, Casino, Castanets, Castle, Catacomb, Catamaran, Catapult, Cataract, Catnip, Cello, Centerfold, Chainsaw, Chandelier, Chaperone, Chariot, Checkbook, Cheerleader, Chess, Chisel, Chiropractor, Chloroform, Chopsticks, Clarinet, Cleaver, Clock, Clodhoppers, Clone, Clorox, Closet, Clown, Club, College, Combat, Comics, Commode, Compass, Computer, Concert, Condo, Confetti, Congress, Convertible, Convoy, Cookbook, Corkscrew, Corral, Coronary, Corset, Corvette, Costume, Cradle, Crib, Croquet, Crossbow, Crowbar, Crown, Cruise, Crutches, Cummerbund, Curfew, Cuspidor, Cutlass, Cyclone, Cymbal, Czar.

D Pegs:	Dachshund, Dalmatian, Damselfish, Damselfly, Deer, Deerfly, Deerhound, Deer Mouse, Devilfish, Diamondback, Dik-dik, Dingo, Dinosaur, Discus, Doberman, Doe, Dog, Dolphin, Donkey, Dormouse, Dove, Dragonfly, Drake, Duck, Duck-billed Platypus, Duckling, Dungeness crab.
D Pivots:	Dagger, Daiquiri, Dandruff, Dart, Daycare, Deadbolt, Decorator, Decoy, Defoliant, Defroster, Degree, Dementia, Derringer, Derby, Deutschemark, Dexedrine, Diabetes, Diamonds, Diapers, Diarrhea, Diary, Dictionary, Diesel, Dinghy, Diploma, Dipstick, Dirigible, Discus, Disease, Disguise, Dishtowel, Diving Board, Divorce, Dobro, Doll House, Doorbell, Doorknob, Dormitory, Dragster, Drama, Drano, Drapes, Drawers, Dress, Dress Code, Drill, Drone, Drought, Drum, Dulcimer, Dumpster, Dump Truck, Dungarees, Dungeon Dynamite.
E Pegs:	Eagle, Eaglet, Earthworm, Earring, Earthquake, Ebola, Eel, Eel Worm, Egret, Eland, Electric Eel, Elephant, Elk, Elephant, Elephant Seal, Elkhound, Emperor Penguin, Emu, English Setter, Ermine, Eskimo Dog, Ewe.
E Pivots:	Earache, Ebola, Effigy, Eggbeater, e-mail, Either, Embassy, Eraser, Escort.

   Caleb Spalding Atwood

F Pegs: Falcon, Fawn, Fer-de-lance, Feral Hog, Ferret, Fiddler crab, Field Mouse, Filly, Finch, Fire ant, Firefly, Fish, Fish Hawk, Flamingo, Flatfish, Flea, Flounder, Fly, Flying fish, Flying Squirrel, Foal, Fox, Hound, Fox Terrier, Frog, Fruit Fly, Fur Seal.

F Pivots: Facebook, Facelift, Facial, Falsies, Fanny pack, Featherbed, Fedora, Ferrari, Ferris Wheel, Fever, Fez, Fiddle, Fiesta, Fife, Filibuster, Filleting knife, Finger paint, Fire alarm, Firecracker, Fire Escape, Fireworks, Flame thrower, Flare, Flask, Flute, Fork, Freezer, Fudge.

G Pegs: Gamecock, Gander, Gar, Garter Snake, Gator, Gazelle, Gecko, Gerbil, German Shepherd, Giant Panda, Giant Squid, Gila monster, Gibbon, Giraffe, Glass fish, Glowworm, Gnat, Gnu, Goat, Golden Eagle, Golden Retriever, Golden Trout, Goldfinch, Goldfish, Goose, Gopher, Gorilla, Grackle, Grasshopper, Gray Fox, Great Dane, Great White Shark, Greyhound, Grizzly bear, Greyhound, Grouper, Grouse, Guide Dog, Guinea Pig, Guppy, Gull, Gypsy Moth.

G Pivots: Gaff, Gag, Gallows, Gallstone, Galoshes, Gang, Gangrene, Garret, Garter Belt, Gas Mask, Gatling Gun, Gavel, Gazebo, Geiger Counter, Glacier, Glider, Glockenspiel, Glue,

Goalpost, Goatee, Google, Goggles, Gold, Golf, Gondola, Grenade, Griddle, Grill, Guillotine, Gunnysack

H Pegs: Haddock, Halibut, Hammerhead, Hamster, Harbor Seal, Hare, Harp Seal, Hartebeest, Hatchet Fish, Hawk, Hawk Owl, Hedgehog, Heifer, Hen, Hermit Crab, Herring, Heron, Hippo, Hog, Holstein, Homing Pigeon, Honey Badger, Honeybee, Hoot Owl, Horned Lark, Hornet, Horse, Horsefly, Howler Monkey, Hummingbird, Humpback, Husky, Hyena.

H Pivots: Haberdasher, Hacienda, Hacksaw, Hailstorm, Haircut, Hairspray, Hairpin, Halitosis, Halo, Hammer, Hammock, Handbag, Handcuffs, Hand Grenade, Handgun, Hangar, Hangover, Halo, Halloween, Happy hour, Harem, Harmonica, Hangar, Hangover, Hanky, Harem, Harmonica, Harness, Harp, Harpoon, Harpsichord, Hatchet, Headlight, Heart Attack, Helicopter, Helmet, Hemlock, Herbicide, Hernia, Hibachi, Hiccups, Highchair, High Heels, Highball, Hip Boots, Hobbyhorse, Hockey, Hoe, Honky-tonk, Hoopskirt, Horoscope, Horseshoe, Horsewhip, Hotrod, Howitzer, Hula Hoop, Hurricane, Hydroplane, Hypnosis.

I Pegs: Ibex, Ibis, Iguana, Impala, Inchworm, Insect, Irish Setter.

Caleb Spalding Atwood

I Pivots: I-beam, Icebox, Ice pick, Ice Rink, Ice Skates, Icicle, Igloo, Incense, Incinerator, Incubator, Inferno, Inflation, Influenza, Inkjet, Inner-tube, Insecticide, Insomnia, Insurance, Intelligence, Interment, Internet, IOU, I-phone.

J Pegs: Jackal, Jackass, Jackrabbit, Jaguar, Jellyfish, June bug.

J Pivots: Jacuzzi, Jack, Jackhammer, Jack-in-the box, Jackknife, Jack-o-lantern, Jackpot, Jacuzzi, Jail, Jalopy, Jaundice, Javelin, Jawbreaker, Jazz, Jellybean, Jester, Jetlag, Jet Ski, Jewelry, Jewels, Jigsaw, Job, Jockey, Jodhpurs, Judo, Jug, Ju-jitsu, Jukebox, Jump Rope, Jumpsuit, Jungle Gym, Gym suit, Jury Duty.

K Pegs: Kangaroo, Kangaroo Bat, Kangaroo Rat, Katydid, Killer Bee, Killer Whale, Komodo Dragon, Kingbird, King Cobra, King Crab, King Fish, King Salmon, King Snake, Kit Fox, Kitten, Kiwi, Koala, Koi, Kookaburra, Krill.

K Pivots: Kaleidoscope, Karate, Kayak, Kazoo, Kerosene, Ketch, Kettle, Kettledrum, Key, Keyboard, Kickback, Kickball, Kiln, Kilt, Kimono, Kite, Kleenex, Kleptomania, K-Mart, Kneepads, Knee Socks, Knife, Kodak, Krugerrand.

L Pegs: Labrador Retriever, Ladybird, Ladybug, Lake Trout, Lamb, Lamprey, Lap Dog, Largemouth Bass, Lark, Leech, Leghorn, Lemming, Lemon Shark, Lemon Sole, Lemur, Leopard, Leopard Seal, Lhasa Apso, Lice, Lightning Bug, Ling, Lion, Lionfish, Lipizzaner, Lizard, Llama, Lobster, Locust, Loggerhead Turtle, Longhorn, Loon, Louse, Love Bird, Lynx.

L Pivots: Laboratory, Lacrosse, Ladder, Ladle, Lamp, Lampshade, Lance, Landfill, Landing Gear, Land Mine, Land slide, Lantern, Lariat, Laryngitis, Laser, Lasso, Latrine, Laughing Gas, Laundromat, Lavatory, Law Degree, Leash, Leotard, Levi, Library, Lie Detector, Lifejacket, Life Raft, Limousine, Lingerie, Lipstick, Literature, Loafers, Lockjaw, Locomotive, Logo, Loincloth, Lollipop, Lottery, Luau, Luger, Leukemia, Lute, Lyricist.

M Pegs: Macaw, Mackerel, Maggot, Magpie, Mako Shark, Malamute, Mallard, Manatee, Mandrill, Man-o-war, Manta Ray, Manx Cat, Mare, Marlin, Marmoset, Martin, Masked booby, Maverick, Mayfly, Meadowlark, Meer Kat, Milk snake, Millipede, Mink, Minnow, Mockingbird, Mole, Mongoose, Mongrel, Monkey, Moose, Mosquito, Moth, Mountain Goat, Mountain Lion, Mourning Dove, Mouse, Mudbug, Mudpuppy, Mule, Mule Deer, Mullet, Musk Ox, Muskrat, Musky, Mussel, Mustang, Myna Bird.

                    Caleb Spalding Atwood

M Pivots: Maalox, Mace, Machete, Makeup, Mandolin, Manicure, Marimba, Marina, Mariachi, Mascara, Mask, Masseuse, Matador, Mazda, Maze, Measles, Megaphone, MENSA, Mentor, Menu, Mercedes, Merry go round, Microphone, Microwave, Migraine, Mini Bike, Miniskirt, Mistletoe, Mittens, Money Belt, Monsoon, Mop, Moped, Morgue, Motorcycle, Mountain Bike, Mousetrap, Mud Flaps, Mug shot, Muffler, Musket, Mustache, Muzzle.

N Pegs: Nanny Goat, Needlefish, Nene, Neon Tetra, Newt, Night Crawler, Night Hawk, Nightingale, Nile Crocodile, Nightingale, Northern Pike, Nutria.

N Pivots: Nails, Nail file, Napalm, Napkin, Narcotics, Nausea, Navigator, Navy, Necklace, Necktie, Negligee, Nerf ball, Net, Newsletter, Nicotine, Nightgown, Nightmare, Nine Iron, Nitroglycerin, Noose, Novel, NRA, NSA, Nuke, Nursemaid.

O Pegs: Ocelot, Octopus, Opossum, Orangutan, Orca, Oriole, Osprey, Ostrich, Otter, Owl, Owlet, Ox, Oyster.

O Pivots: Obituary, Oboe, Odometer, Office, Oil Well, Old Spice, Opal, Opera, Orchestra, Organ, Oscar, Ottoman, Ouija Board, Outhouse, Oven, Overalls, Overcoat, Overshoes..

P Pegs: Packrat, Palomino, Panda, Panther, Parakeet, Parrot, Partridge, Passenger Pigeon, Peacock, Peahen, Peccary, Pekinese, Pelican, Penguin, Perch, Peregrine, Persian Cat, Pheasant, Pickerel, Pig, Pigeon, Piglet, Pygmy Whale, Pike, Pinto, Pilot fish, Pilot Whale, Piranha, Pit Bull, Platypus, Polecat, Polar Bear, Polecat, Pollywog, Pomeranian, Pompano, Pony, Poodle, Porcupine, Porpoise, Possum, Potbellied Pig, Prairie Chicken, Prairie Dog, Prawn, Praying Mantas, Pronghorn, Puff Adder, Puffer Fish, Puffin, Pug, Pullet, Puma, Puppy, Python.

P Pivots: Pacifier, Paddle, Pager, Paintbrush, Pajamas, Pantaloons, Pantyhose, Parachute, Paralysis, Parasol, Parole, Passport, Pawnshop, Peashooter, Pedigree, Penthouse, Perfume, Peroxide, Petticoat, Ph.D. Piano, Piccolo, Pick axe Pile Driver, Pinafore, Ping Pone, Pistol, Pitchfork, Plow, Pogo Stick, Polo, Poncho, Pop Gun, Porsche, Powder Puff, Prison, Propeller, Publicity, Punchbowl, Purse, Putter, Puzzle, Pyromania.

Q Pegs: Quahog, Quail, Quarter Horse.

Q Pivots: Quagmire, Quarrel, Quarterback, Quicksand, Quilt, Quiver, Quonset Hut.

R Pegs: Rabbit, Raccoon, Ram, Raptor, Rat, Rattlesnake, Raven, Ray, Razorback, Red Ant, Red

Caleb Spalding Atwood

Bird, Redfish, Red Fox, Red Snapper, Red Wolf, Reef Shark, Reindeer, Rhesus Monkey, Rhino, Ribbonfish, Ridley Turtle, River Otter, Roach, Roadrunner, Robin, Rock Bass, Rock Lobster, Rodent, Rooster, Rottweiler.

R Pivots:	Rabies, Radar, Radio, Raft, Raincoat, Rake, Rasp, Rattle, Razor, Reel, Regatta, Resume, Revolver, Rickshaw, Rifle, Rickshaw, Roadster, Rocker, Rocket, Rodeo, Rollercoaster, Rolls Royce, Root Canal, Rouge, Roulette, Rowboat, Rudder, Rugby.
S Pegs:	Sable, Sailfish, Saint Bernard, Salamander, Salmon, Sand Fly, Sand Hill Crane, Sandpiper, Sardine, Scallop, Schnauzer, Scorpion, Scotty, Screech Owl, Scrod, Seagull, Seahawk, Seahorse, Seal, Sea Lion, Sea Otter, Sea Slug, Sea Trout, Sea Urchin, Seeing-eye Dog, Shallot, Shark, Sheep, Sheepdog, Sheltie, Sidewinder, Shrimp, Silkworm.
S Pivots:	Saber, Saddle, Saddlebag, Safari, Sailboat, Sarong, Sash, Sauna, Sawhorse, Saxophone, Scalpel, Scissors, Scooter, Scow, Scurvy, Seatbelt, Seesaw, Settee, Shillelagh, Shot put, Shotgun, Shovel, Sickle, Silly putty, Sitar, Skateboard, Ski, Skillet, Skirt, Sledgehammer, Slingshot, Slot Machine, Snare, Snorkel, Snow Ploy, Soapbox, Soccer, Socks, Softball, Software, Sombrero, Sonar, Spa, Spaceship,

Spanish, Sparkplug, Spats, Spatula, Spear, Speedboat, Speedometer, Spitball, Spittoon, Spotlight, Spurs, Steamboat, Stereo, Stiletto, Stilts, Stockcar, Stradivari, Straightjacket, Stirrup, Strychnine, Submarine, Superglue, Suspenders, Sweat Socks, Swimsuit, Stick, Sword.

T Pegs:

Tabby Cat, Tadpole, Tilapia, Tapeworm, Tapir, Tarantula, Tarpon. Tasmanian Devil, Teal, Termite, Tic, Tiger, Tiger Shark, Timber Wolf, Titmouse, Toad, Tomcat, Tortoise, Toucan, Tree Toad, Triggerfish, Trout, Trumpeter Swan, Tsetse Fly, Tuna, Turkey, Turkey Buzzard, Turtle dove.

T Pivots:

Tack Hammer, Tailor, Tambourine, Tape Deck, Tar Pit, Tattoo, Teargas, Telephone, Telescope, Television, Tennis, Tepee, Tiddlywinks, Tights, Tightrope, Time Bomb, Tinker Toy, Tires, TNT, Toboggan, Tow-tag, Tomahawk, Tommy Gun, Tom-tom, Toothache, Tool kit, Torch, Toreador, Tornado, Torpedo, Totem pole, Toupee, Trampoline, Trapeze, Tricycle, Trousers, Troubadour, Truck, Trumpet, Tsunami, Tuba, Tugboat, Tuxedo, Twister, Twitter, Typhoon,

U Pegs:

Umbrella Bird.

U Pivots:

Ukulele, Ulcer, Underwear, Union, University, Umbrella, Umpire.

					Caleb Spalding Atwood

V Pegs:	Varmint, Vampire Bat, Vicuna, Viper, Vole, Vulture.
V Pivots:	Garment, Tuna, Diaper, Garment, Pole, Culture.
W Pegs:	Wallaby, Wasp, Wildcat, Weasel, Whale, Walrus, Woodcock, Wolf,
W Pivots:	Wallet, Waltz, Warden, Wardrobe, Whiskey, Wine,
X Pegs:	Xray Tetra, Xanthus,
X Pivots:	Nil
Y Pegs:	Yak, Yellow billed stork, Yellow Mongoose.
Y Pivots:	Yak, Yacht, Yardstick
Z Pegs	Zebra, Zorilla
Z Pivots:	Zipper, Zircon, Zoo

APPENDIX B

RHYMING QUIPS

A RHYMING QUIP OPTIONS

Aardvark: Amusement park, ballpark, Cutty Sark, Deutschemark: ear mark, lark, Makers Mark, meadowlark, monarch, national park, shark, skylark, theme park, tiger shark

Abalone: alimony, macaroni, matrimony, palimony, pepperoni, pony, spumoni

Adder: bladder, ladder, step ladder.

Airedale: brail, Clydesdale, coattail, cocktail, cottontail, e-mail, fairytale, ginger ale, hangnail, jail, junk mail, killer whale, monorail, nail mail, nail, nightingale, pigtail, pilot whale, ponytail, pygmy whale, quail, sail, scale, snail, snail mail, sperm whale, tattletale, vapor trail, veil, voicemail, beluga whale, whale

Akita: cheetah, fajita, margarita, senorita.

Albacore: ambassador, bed sore, boar, book store, commodore, condor, cuspidor, drug store, fire door, humidor, Labrador, liquor store, man-o-war, matador, mentor, memoir, oar, parquet floor, picador, pinafore, raptor, realtor, revolving door, saddle sore, storm door, swinging door, toreador, troubadour, war

Albatross: boss, dental floss, lacrosse, moss, motor cross, pit boss, straw boss

Alligator: accelerator, arbitrator, aviator, calculator, carburetor, crater, decorator, detonator, dumb waiter, escalator, elevator, exterminator, radiator, prevaricator, refrigerator, tailgater, vibrator

Alpaca: nil

Amoeba: Margarita, zebra

Anaconda: Honda, Uganda, veranda

Anchovy: nil+

Angelfish: baking dish, billfish, catfish, codfish, crawfish, damselfish, death wish, devilfish, fetish, goldfish, jellyfish, kingfish, lionfish, Petri dish, redfish, rockfish, sailfish, satellite dish, sawfish, shellfish, soap dish, sunfish, swordfish, triggerfish, whitefish, Yiddish

 Caleb Spalding Atwood

Angleworm: accounting firm, germ, law firm, pachy-
                    derm, perm, prison term, pachyderm

Angora Goat: banknote, C-note, coyote, creosote,
                    dreamboat, ferryboat, gunboat, houseboat,
                    iceboat, lab coat, lifeboat, mountain goat,
                    nanny goat, pea coat, petticoat, rowboat,
                    sailboat, speedboat, steamboat, strep
                    throat, T-note, torpedo boat, trench coat,
                    tugboat, U-boat, vote

Ant: assailant, confidant, consultant, defoliant,
                    deodorant, fire ant hydrant, implant, intox-
                    icant, pendant, power plant, spider plant,
                    stretch pant, transplant

Anteater: Beefeater, egg beater, heater, two-seater.

Antelope: bunny slope, gyroscope, horoscope, jump
                    rope, kaleidoscope, microscope, periscope,
                    stethoscope, telescope, tight rope

Ape: adhesive tape, audiotape, cape, drape, duct
                    tape, fire escape, masking tape, red tape,
                    Scotch tape, tickertape, videotape

Archerfish: see Angelfish

Armadillo: cigarillo, peccadillo, pillow, willow

Asp: clasp, handclasp, rasp

Ass: bass, bluegrass, brass, crabgrass, gas, glass,
                    jackass, salt grass, sassafras, sea bass, shot

glass, spyglass, stained glass, teargas, laughing gas, lemongrass, wineglass

B RHYMING QUIP OPTIONS

Baboon: bassoon, balloon, buffoon, cartoon, cocoon, coon, goon, greasy spoon, harpoon, honeymoon, lagoon, loon, monsoon, pantaloon, platoon, pontoon, raccoon, saloon, sand dune, silver spoon, spittoon, trial balloon, tycoon, typhoon

Badger: nil

Bald Eagle: illegal, legal, regal

Barn Owl: fowl, hoot owl, howl, towel

Barnacle: nil

Barracuda: Bermuda, Buddha

Bass: bluegrass, brass, crabgrass, gas, glass, jackass, salt grass, sassafras, sea bass, shot glass, spyglass, stained glass, teargas, laughing gas, lemongrass, wineglass

Basset Hound: Afghan hound, battleground,

Bloodhound, dachshund, deer hound, dog pound, fairground, fox hound, greyhound, lost and found, *merry*-go-round, muscle bound, parade ground, playground, surround sound, ultrasound hound, wolfhound

 Caleb Spalding Atwood

Bat:

alley cat, autocrat, bobcat, bureaucrat, calico cat, combat, coolie hat, copycat, cowboy hat, dingbat, diplomat, doormat, fungo bat, hard hat, mud flap, muskrat, place mat, polecat, porkpie hat, rat, rheostat, Siamese cat, silk hat, tabby cat, technocrat, Savannah cat, tomcat, top hat, vampire bat, welcome mat, wildcat, wombat

Beagle:

illegal, legal, regal

Bear:

air fare, armchair, boutonniere, chair, electric chair, day care, fair, flare, hare, highchair, lawn chair, potty-chair, mare, Medicare, polar bear, rocking chair, silverware, snare, software, swivel chair, underwear, welfare, wheelchair

Beaver:

cantilever, cleaver, fever, golden retriever, Labrador reliever, weaver, wide receiver

Bedbug:

bear hug, beer mug, coffee mug, fireplug, jitterbug, ladybug, lightning bug, litterbug, oriental rug, prayer rug, Sea Slug, spark plug.

Bee:

BB, bumblebee, artillery, bikini, biscotti, Chablis, chamois, chili, chimpanzee, Christmas tree, church key, college degree, daiquiri, DDT, epee, factory, fee, Ferrari, fleur-de-lis, Frisbee, goatee, golf tee, graffiti, grease monkey, greens fee, hemlock tree, hibachi, honeybee, husky, iced tea, jamboree, killer bee, kiti, kiwi, law degree, lingerie, LSD, machete, maitre d', manatee, martini, pass key, pedigree, privy, referee, renminbi, rotisserie, Saki, shoe tree, skeleton key, snow ski, spaghetti, squeegee, tepee, TNT, trick knee, water ski

Bighorn:	bullhorn, English horn, flugelhorn, foghorn, French horn, greenhorn, leghorn, longhorn, morn, popcorn, powder horn, saddle horn, shoehorn, thorn, uniform

Billy Goat:	see Angora goat

Bird:	blackbrd, bluebird, buzzword, crossword, dodo bird, hummingbird, jailbird, mockingbird, password, redbird, swearword, Thunderbird, whirlybird

Birddog:	blog, bulldog, bullfrog, catalog, frog, grog, groundhog, guide dog, hog, leapfrog, pollywog, prairie dog, sheepdog, smog, travelogue, tree frog, warthog, Yule log

Bison:	nil

Black Drum:	atrium, asylum, conundrum, drum, kettle drum, rum, tantrum

Black lab:	cab, crab, flab crime lab, fiddler crab, gift of gab, horseshoe crab, king crab, science lab, space lab, taxicab

Blackbird: see Bird

Bloodhound: see Basset Hound

Blue jay: ash tray, attaché, ballet, beret, bidet, bou-
                      quet, cabaret, cabernet, café, chalet,
                      Chevrolet, croquet, flight pay, hair spray,
                      jay, manta ray, moray, negligee, Nene, os-
                      prey, pepper spray, sleigh, stingray, subway,
                      toupee, Valentine's day.

Blue Whale: see Airedale

Bluebird: see Bird

Bluefish: see Angelfish

Bluegill: chill, fire drill, gerbil, grille, krill, landfill,
                      molehill, oil spill, pepper mill, pep pill,
                      poison pill, quill, road kill, saw mill,
                      Spoonbill Cat, swill, T-bill, treadmill,
                      whippoorwill, Will, windmill

Boa: aloha, Mauna Loa, protozoa

Boar: ambassador, bed sore, boar, book store,
                      commodore, condor, cuspidor, drug store,
                      fire door, humidor, Labrador, liquor store,
                      man-o-war, matador, mentor, memoir, oar,
                      parquet floor, picador, pinafore, raptor, re-
                      altor, revolving door, saddle sore, storm
                      door, swinging door, toreador, troubadour,
                      war

Bobcat:

alley cat, bat, cat, gat, hat, rat, spat, vat, alley cat, autocrat, bat, bobcat, bureaucrat, calico cat, combat, coolie hat, copycat, cowboy hat, dingbat, diplomat, doormat, fungo bat, hard hat, laundromat, mud flaps, muskrat, place mat, polecat, porkpie hat, rat, rheostat, Siamese cat, silk hat, tabby cat, technocrat, Savannah cat, tomcat, top hat, vampire bat, welcome mat, wildcat, wombat

Bonefish:

see Angelfish

Bonito:

incognito, veto

Border Collie:

dolly, jolly, trolley, tea trolley, folly, volley

Boxer:

nil

Bronco:

air show, art deco, backhoe, bronco, buffalo, bungalow, cash flow, cello, chapeau, chateau, crossbow, crow, doe, dog and pony show, domino, echo, escrow, free throw, gazebo, halo, hoe, inferno, longbow, mango, minnow, mistletoe, mosquito, oboe, Oleo, Oreo, peep show, piccolo, radio, rainbow, rhino, rodeo, scarecrow, ski tow, skid row, sparrow, standing O, stereo, tennis elbow, TKO, trousseau, volcano, widow

Brook trout:

drought, gout, knockout, bailout, boy scout, brown trout, cookout, cutthroat

Caleb Spalding Atwood

trout, cub scout, downspout, dugout, Eagle scout, girl scout, golden trout, gout, knockout, lake trout, pitchout, rainbow trout, rainout, sea trout, speckled trout, strikeout.

Buck: beginner's luck, buzzard's luck, duck, dump truck, fire truck, hockey puck, pickup truck, sawbuck, tow truck

Buffalo: incognito, veto

Bug: bear hug, beer mug, coffee mug, fireplug, jitterbug, ladybug, lightning bug, litterbug, oriental rug, prayer rug, Sea Slug, spark plug

Bull Moose: abuse, caboose, calaboose, fruit juice, juice, masseuse, goose, mongoose, noose, papoose, produce, prune juice, snow goose

Bull: pit bull, steel wool, taffy pull

Bulldog: see Bird dog

Bullfrog: see Bulldog.

Bumblebee: see Bee.

Bunny: dust bunny, funny money, honey, hush money, pin money

Burro: nil

Bushmaster: brew master, broadcaster, concertmaster, disaster, forecaster, mustard plaster, news-

caster, sand blaster, sportscaster, toastmas-
ter, quartermaster, telecaster, weathercaster

Butterfly: alibi, apple pie, barfly, battle cry, black eye,
bolo tie, bow tie, buckeye, cow pie, dead-
eye, dragonfly, electric eye, FBI, firefly,
gadfly, GI, hawk eye, hi-fi, jai-alai, lullaby,
magpie, mai tai, necktie, pig sty, pinkeye,
private eye, railroad tie, RBI, semi, string
tie, tie dye, sty, tsetse fly, walleye

Buzzard: nil

C RHYMING QUIP OPTIONS

Calamari: actuary, adversary, beneficiary, Bloody
Mary, canary, confectionary, coronary,
dairy, dictionary, fairy, ferry, fiduciary, itinerary, judiciary, library, military, monastery,
mortuary, peccary, secretary, Stradivari,
sherry, stationary, tooth fairy

Calf: carafe, cardiograph, decaf, flagstaff, gaffe,
giraffe, hovercraft, phonograph, telegraph,
sales staff

Calico Cat: alley cat, autocrat, bobcat, bureaucrat,
combat, coolie hat, copycat, cowboy hat,
dingbat, diplomat, doormat, fungo bat,
hard hat, Laundromat, mud flap, muskrat,
place mat, polecat, porkpie hat, rat, rheo-

stat, Siamese cat, silk hat, tabby cat, technocrat, Savannah cat, tomcat, top hat, vampire bat, welcome mat, wildcat, wombat

Camel: mammal, enamel

Canary: actuary, adversary, beneficiary, Bloody Mary, confectionary, coronary, dairy, dictionary, fairy, ferry, fiduciary, itinerary, judiciary, library, military, monastery, mortuary, peccary, secretary, Stradivari, sherry, stationary, tooth fairy

Cardinal: affordable, convertible, farcical, remarkable, workable

Caribou: barbecue, brew, canoe, cockatoo, cork screw, ewe, gnu, hairdo, horse shoe, igloo, IOU, kangaroo, kazoo, microbrew, shampoo, tattoo, tofu, voodoo, Waterloo

Carp: autoharp, harp, tarp

Carrier Pigeon: clay pigeon, homing pigeon, passenger pigeon, religion, stool pigeon

Cat: alley cat, bat, cat, gat, hat, rat, spat, vat, alley cat, autocrat, bat, bobcat, bureaucrat, calico cat, combat, coolie hat, copycat, cowboy hat, dingbat, diplomat, doormat, fungo bat, hard hat, laundromat, mud flap, muskrat, place mat, polecat, porkpie hat, rat, rheostat, Siamese cat, silk hat, tabby cat, technocrat, Savannah cat, tomcat, top hat, vampire bat, welcome mat, wildcat, wombat

Caterpillar: distiller, driller, griller, killer, pain killer, Rototiller, weed killer

Catfish: see Angelfish

Centipede: bead, birdseed, chicken feed, duckweed, hayseed, millipede, nosebleed, poppy seed, screed, seaweed, stampede

Chamois: BB, bumblebee, artillery, bikini, biscotti, Chablis, chili, chimpanzee, Christmas tree, church key, college degree, daiquiri, DDT, epee, factory, fee, Ferrari, fleur-de-lis, Frisbee, goatee, golf tee, graffiti, grease monkey, greens fee, hemlock tree, hibachi, honeybee, husky, iced tea, jamboree, killer bee, kiti, kiwi, law degree, lingerie, LSD, machete, maître d', manatee, martini, pass key, pedigree, privy, referee, renminbi, rotisserie, Saki, shoe tree, skeleton key, snow ski, spaghetti, squeegee, tepee, TNT, trick knee, water ski

Cheetah: Akita, cheetah, fajita, margarita, senorita

Cheshire Cat: alley cat, bat, cat, gat, hat, rat, spat, vat, alley cat, autocrat, bat, bobcat, bureaucrat, calico cat, combat, coolie hat, copycat, cowboy hat, dingbat, diplomat, doormat, hard hat, laundromat, mud flap, muskrat, place mat, polecat, porkpie hat, rat, rheostat, Siamese cat, silk hat, tabby cat, technocrat, Savannah cat, tomcat, top hat, vampire bat, welcome mat, wildcat, wombat

Chick: chopstick, dipstick, dik-dik, drumstick, gold brick, hat trick, ice pick, kick, lipstick, oil slick, pick, place kick, salt lick, sidekick, stick, tick, toothpick, yardstick, candlestick, pogo stick, swizzle stick

Chickadee: see Bee.

Chicken: awestricken, panic stricken, poverty stricken, prairie chicken, spring chicken

Chihuahua: nil

Chimpanzee: see Bee.

Chinchilla: flotilla, gorilla, guerilla, hydrilla, sarsaparilla, villa, vanilla

Chipmunk: bunk, drunk, junk, Podunk, skunk, slam dunk, steamer trunk, trunk

Cicada: Grenada

Clam: battering ram, cardiogram, exam, grand slam, hologram, lamb, monogram, mammogram, ram, scam, sky cam, spam, telegram, tinker's damn, traffic jam, web cam

Clownfish: see Angelfish

Clydesdale: brail, coattail, cocktail, cocktail, cottontail, e-mail, fairytale, ginger ale, hangnail, jail, junk mail, killer whale, monorail, nail mail, nail, nightingale, pigtail, pilot whale, ponytail, pygmy whale, quail, sail, scale, snail, snail mail, sperm whale, tattletale, vapor trail, veil, voicemail, beluga whale, whale

Cobra: coma, diploma, Toyota, viola, yoga

Cockatiel: automobile, bookmobile, buffing wheel, curb appeal, eel, elephant seal, Ferris wheel, flywheel, glockenspiel, harp seal, leopard seal, paddle wheel, seal, spinning wheel, stiletto heel

Cockatoo: barbecue, brew, canoe, cockatoo, cork screw, ewe, gnu, hairdo, horse shoe, igloo, IOU, kangaroo, kazoo, microbrew, shampoo, tattoo, tofu, voodoo, Waterloo

Cocker Spaniel: Brittany Spaniel, Springer spaniel

Cockroach: coach, poach, encroach, brooch, coach, roach, stagecoach

Cod: Cape Cod, divining rod, façade, firing squad, lightning rod, scrod, vice squad

Coho: hobo, logo, oboe, polo, Volvo, yoyo,

Collie: border collie, dolly, folly, trolley, tea trolley, volley

    Caleb Spalding Atwood

Colt: dead bolt, lag bolt, revolt, thunderbolt, toggle bolt

Condor: ambassador, cuspidor, door, humidor, matador, picador

Coon: baboon, bassoon, balloon, cartoon, cocoon, harpoon, honeymoon, monsoon, pantaloon, raccoon, swoon, tycoon, typhoon,

Coonhound: see basset hound

Copperhead: bedspread, blockhead, bobsled, bonehead, bread, bunk bed, cornbread, dogsled, featherbed, gingerbread, hammerhead, moped, rose bed, steelhead thoroughbred, tool shed, twin bed, water bed

Coral Snake: air brake, backache, bellyache, birthday cake, coffee break, disc brake, earthquake, emergency brake, fruitcake, garter snake, green snake, grubstake, hand brake, king snake, parking brake, rattlesnake, sea snake, snake, snow flake, tax break, wedding cake

Cormorant: see Ant

Cottonmouth: big mouth, motor-mouth.

Cottontail: brail, Clydesdale, coattail, cocktail, cocktail, e-mail, fairytale, ginger ale, hangnail, jail, junk mail, killer whale, monorail, nail mail, nail, nightingale, pigtail, pilot whale, ponytail, pygmy whale, quail, sail, scale, snail, snail mail, sperm whale, tattletale, vapor trail, veil, voicemail, beluga whale, whale

Cougar:
computer, cruiser, looter, luger, neuter, scooter, suitor, tutor

Cow:
chow, frau, hausfrau, hoosegow, luau, plow, powwow, scow, plow

Cowbird:
bluebird, buzzword, crossword, humming-bird, mockingbird, password, redbird, swearword, Thunderbird, whirlybird, jail-bird

Coyote:
See Bee.

Crab:
black lab, cab, flab crime lab, fiddler crab, gift of gab, horseshoe crab, king crab, science lab, space lab, taxicab

Crappie:
See Bee.

Crawdad:
Hot pad, undergrad, kneepad, launch pad, scratch pad, shad, shoulder pad.

Crayfish:
see Angelfish

Cricket:
parking ticket, pawn ticket, picket, speeding ticket, sticky wicket

Croc:
acid rock, alarm clock, Bach, butcher-block, chopping block, cuckoo clock,

dreadlock, flintlock, frock, grandfather
clock, hemlock, padlock, peacock, penny
stock, poppycock, punk rock, Reebok,
shellshock, shock jock, shot clock, shuttle-
cock, smock, springbok, sweat sock, time
clock, windsock, wok, woodcock

Crocodile: circular file, domicile, hair style, nail file, smile, sundial, turnstile

Crow: air show, art deco, backhoe, bronco, buffalo, bungalow, cash flow, cello, chapeau, chateau, crossbow, doe, dog and pony show, domino, echo, escrow, free throw, gazebo, halo, hoe, inferno, longbow, mango, minnow, mistletoe, mosquito, oboe, Oleo, Oreo, peep show, piccolo, radio, rainbow, rhino, rodeo, scarecrow, ski tow, skid row, sparrow, standing O, stereo, tennis elbow, TKO, trousseau, volcano, widow

Cub: club, grub, nub, pub, sub, tub

D RHYMING QUIP OPTIONS

Dachshund: cummerbund, fund, refund

Dalmatian: adoration, annihilation, aggravation, animation, arbitration, asphyxiation, beautification, coeducation, constipation, contamination,

coronation, corporation, decoration, detoxi-
fication, denigration, deodorization, depra-
vation, desolation, dictation, education,
electrification, elongation, gas station, hiber-
nation, inebriation, insulation, litigation, sex
education, space station, starvation, strangu-
lation, taxation, transportation, vocation.

Damsel Fly: see Butterfly

Damselfish: see Angelfish

Deer: beer, boutonniere, brassiere, cauliflower
                  ear, cashier, chandelier, charioteer, civil en-
                  gineer, gondolier, headgear, landing gear,
                  musketeer, peer, puppeteer, reindeer
                  Shakespeare, spear, steer, tapir

Deerfly: see Butterfly

Deerhound: see Basset hound

Devilfish: see Angelfish

Diamond-back: backpack, blackjack, bootblack, bric-a-
                  brac, Cadillac, cognac, gunnysack, hatch-
                  back, ice pack, gunny sack, hatchback,
                  heart attack, kayak, knapsack, Muzak,
                  Prozac, racetrack, silverback, racetrack, ra-
                  zorback, setback, six-pack, ski rack, smoke-
                  stack, tarmac, thumbtack, tie rack, yak

Dik-dik: chopstick, dipstick, drumstick, gold brick,
                  hat trick, ice pick, kick, lipstick, oil slick,

              Caleb Spalding Atwood

pick, place kick, salt lick, sidekick, stick, tick, toothpick, yardstick, candlestick, pogo stick, swizzle stick

Dingo: bingo, flamingo

Dinosaur: book store, drugstore, humidor, matador, troubadour

Discus: nil

Doberman: bedpan, caravan, caveman, doorman, frying pan, sedan, toucan

Dodo bird: see Bird

Doe: air show, art deco, backhoe, bronco, buffalo, bungalow, cash flow, cello, chapeau, chateau, crossbow, crow, doe, dog and pony show, domino, echo, escrow, free throw, gazebo, halo, hoe, inferno, longbow, mango, minnow, mistletoe, mosquito, oboe, Oleo, Oreo, peep show, piccolo, radio, rainbow, rhino, rodeo, scarecrow, ski tow, skid row, sparrow, standing O, stereo, tennis elbow, TKO, trousseau, volcano, widow

Dog: bird dog, blog, bullfrog, catalog, dog, frog, grog, groundhog, hog, leapfrog, pollywog, prairie dog, sheepdog, smog, travelogue, tree frog, warthog, Yule log

Dolphin: gin, bobby pin, cave-in, clothespin, coonskin, cotton gin, dustbin, gin, hairpin, pigskin, Ritalin, rolling pin, safety pin, sea urchin, sheepskin, sloe gin, tenpin, violin

Donkey: See Bee.

Dormouse: alehouse, beach house, blouse, bunkhouse, clubhouse, deer mouse, dog house, doll house, field mouse, flophouse, grouse, guardhouse, hen house, jailhouse, lighthouse, louse, opera house, penthouse, slaughter house, smokehouse, statehouse, titmouse

Dove: boxing glove, foxglove, golf glove, kidglove, love, mourning dove, puppy love, white glove.

Dover sole: bankroll, cruise control, foxhole, punchbowl, remote control, rock and roll, totem pole

Draft Horse: Arabian horse, air force, charley horse, clotheshorse, divorce, golf course, hobbyhorse, obstacle course, quarter horse, racecourse, sawhorse, seahorse, task force

Dragonfly: see Butterfly

Drake: air brake, backache, bellyache, birthday cake, coffee break, coral snake, disc brake, earthquake, emergency brake, fruitcake, garter snake, green snake, grubstake, hand brake, king snake, parking brake, rattlesnake, sea snake, snake, snow flake, tax break, wedding cake

        Caleb Spalding Atwood

Duck: beginner's luck, buzzard's luck, dump truck, fire truck, hockey puck, pickup truck, sawbuck, tow truck

Duckling: boxing ring, engagement ring, king, shoe-string, sling, string, swing, teething ring, wedding ring

E RHYMING QUIP OPTIONS

Eagle: bald eagle, beagle, illegal, legal, paralegal, regal.

Eaglet: bassinet, bayonet, briquette, cigarette, clarinet, coronet, Corvette, debt, dip net, egret, ink-jet, jet, minuet, mullet, rocket, roulette, tea set, videocassette

Earthworm: see Angleworm

Eel: automobile, bookmobile, buffing wheel, cockatiel, curb appeal, eel, elephant seal, Ferris wheel, flywheel, glockenspiel, harp seal, leopard seal, paddle wheel, seal, spinning wheel, stiletto heel

Egret: bassinet, bayonet, briquette, cigarette, clarinet, coronet, Corvette, debt, dip net, egret, ink-jet, jet, minuet, mullet, rocket, roulette, tea set, videocassette

Eland: Baby Grand, band, bandstand, brand, brass

	band, deckhand, Dixie land, grandstand, jug band, Krugerrand, quicksand, taxi stand
Electric Eel:	see Eel
Elephant:	bunt, cold front, foxhunt, manhunt, scavenger hunt, witch hunt
Elk:	nil
Elkhound:	see Basset Hound
Emu:	barbecue, brew, canoe, cockatoo, cork screw, ewe, gnu, hairdo, horse shoe, igloo, IOU, kangaroo, kazoo, micro-brew, shampoo, tattoo, tofu, voodoo, Waterloo
English Setter:	chain letter, debtor, fan letter, go-getter, jet-setter, newsletter, pacesetter
Ermine:	sermon, German, vermin
Eskimo Dog:	blog, bulldog, bullfrog, catalog, dog, frog, grog, groundhog, guide dog, hog, leapfrog, pollywog, prairie dog, sheepdog, smog, travelogue, tree frog, warthog, Yule log
Ewe:	See Caribou.

F RHYMING QUIP OPTIONS

| Falcon: | nil |
| Fawn: | baton, brawn, pawn, solon, swan, yawn |

     Caleb Spalding Atwood

Ferret: demerit, garret, merit, parrot

Filly: See Bee.

Finch: inch, cinch, clinch, lynch, pinch, winch

Fire Ant: see Ant

Firefly: see Butterfly

Fish: see Angelfish

Flamingo: bingo, dingo, lingo

Flatfish: see Angelfish

Fly: see Butterfly

Flying Fish: see Angelfish

Foal: bankroll, cruise control, flagpole, foxhole,
                         Dover sole, manhole, oriole, parole,
                         punchbowl

Fox Hound: see Basset hound

Fox Terrier: aircraft carrier, wind barrier, derriere

Fox: arctic Fox, ballot box, bobby socks, boom box,
                         boondocks, Botox, dreadlocks, flintlocks,
                         grandfather clocks, idiot box, jack-in-the-box,
                         jukebox, mailbox, musk ox, ox, Pandora's box,
                         pillbox, press box, safe deposit box, sandbox,
                         shamrocks, shot clocks, shuttlecocks, skybox,
                         smallpox, soapbox, socks, squawk box, stocks,
                         strongbox, toolbox, Xerox

Frog: bird dog, blog, bullfrog, catalog, dog, grog, groundhog, hog, leapfrog, pollywog, prairie dog, sheepdog, smog, travelogue, tree frog, warthog, Yule log

Fruit Fly: see Butterfly

G RHYMING QUIP OPTIONS

Gamecock: baby talk, chicken hawk, cakewalk, clock, cuckoo clock, deadlock, double talk, dreadlock, fish hawk, flintlock, hammerlock, hawk, hemlock, lock, moonwalk, mosquito hawk, night hawk, padlock, peacock, pigeon hawk, pillow talk, tomahawk, war hawk, wedlock, wok, woodcock

Gander: commander, dander, salamander

Gar: armoire, armored car, bazaar, boudoir, boxcar, bumper car, candy bar, cattle car, cigar, crowbar, czar, film star, freight car, gar, guitar, jaguar, muscle car, pace car, radar, side car, sitar, scar, sleeping car, sonar, sports car, squad car, steel guitar, tank car, T-bar, tool bar, muscle car, pace car, pine tar, sleeping car, sonar steel guitar, streetcar, squad car, VCR, wine bar, wrecking bar

Gator: aviator, carburetor, escalator, gladiator,

Gazelle: barbell, bombshell, carousel, cowbell, motel

Gecko: libretto, stiletto

Giant Panda: Panda, propaganda, veranda,

Giant Squid: see Captain Kidd, Madrid, power grid, skid, squid

Gila Monster: coiffeur, fur, liqueur, raconteur, saboteur, spur

Giraffe: carafe, cardiograph, decaf, flagstaff, gaffe, hovercraft, phonograph, telegraph, sales staff

Glassfish: see Angelfish

Glowworm: see Angleworm

Gnat: see Alley Cat.

Gnu: caribou, corkscrew, kazoo, menu, zoo

Goat: see Angora Goat

Golden Eagle: illegal, legal, regal

Goldfinch: inch, cinch, pinch

Goldfish: see Angelfish

Goose: see Bull Moose

Gopher: chauffer, loafer

Gorilla: see Chinchilla.

Gosling: boxing ring, engagement ring, king, shoe-
                  string, sling, string, swing, teething ring,
                  wedding ring

Grackle: debacle, jackal, tackle, tabernacle debacle

Grasshopper: chopper, clodhopper, eavesdropper, eye-
                  dropper, flip flopper, hip hopper, share-
                  cropper, teenybopper, topper

Gray Wolf: Beowulf, gray wolf, red wolf, timber wolf

Great Dane: airplane, champagne, crane, migraine, pain

Green Snake: air brake, backache, bellyache, birthday
                  cake, coffee break, disc brake, earthquake,
                  emergency brake, fruitcake, garter snake,
                  grubstake, hand brake, king snake, parking
                  brake, rattlesnake, sea snake, snake, snow
                  flake, tax break, wedding cake

Greyhound: see Basset hound

Grizzly Bear: See Bear

Groundhog: blog, bulldog, bullfrog, catalog, dog, frog,
                  grog, hog, leapfrog, pollywog, prairie dog,
                  sheepdog, smog, travelogue, tree frog,
                  warthog, Yule log see Birddog

Grouper: blooper, paratrooper, party-pooper,
                  pooper-scooper, snooper, state trooper,
                  storm trooper

Grouse: alehouse, beach house, blouse, bunkhouse,

clubhouse, deer mouse, dog house, doll
house, dormouse, field mouse, flophouse,
grouse, guardhouse, hen house, jailhouse,
lighthouse, louse, mouse, opera house,
penthouse, slaughter house, smokehouse,
statehouse, titmouse

Guinea Pig: bigwig, brig, gig, jury-rig, pot-bellied pig,
powdered wig, shindig, sprig, trig,
whirligig, wig

Gull: scull, seagull, skull.

Guppy: puppy, mud puppy, yuppie

H RHYMING QUIP OPTIONS

Halibut: buzz cut, cigar butt, coconut, crew cut,
haircut, lug nut, mutt, rotgut, scuttlebutt,
short put, wing nut

Hammerhead: see Copperhead

Hamster: nil

Hare: air fare, armchair, boutonniere, chair, electric chair, day care, fair, flare, hare, highchair, lawn chair, potty-chair, mare,
Medicare, polar bear, rocking chair, silverware, snare, software, swivel chair, underwear, welfare, wheelchair

Haddock: acid rock, alarm clock, Bach, butcher-block, chopping block, crock, cuckoo clock, dreadlock, flintlock, frock, grandfather clock, hemlock, padlock, peacock, penny stock, poppycock, punk

Harp Seal:	see Cockatiel
Hartebeest:	beat, feast, police
Hatchet Fish:	see Angelfish
Hawk:	see Gamecock
Hedgehog:	see Dog
Heifer:	nil
Hen:	bullpen, fountain pen, hen, peahen, bullpen, carcinogen, comedienne, den, five-and-ten, fox den, fountain pen, playpen, poison pen, RN, Zen, wren
Hermit Crab:	see Crab
Heron:	baron, robber baron
Herring:	boxing ring, engagement ring, king, shoestring, sling, string, swing, teething ring, wedding ring
Hippo:	Zippo
Hog:	see Dog
Holstein:	assembly line, breadline, brine, bust line, carbine, chorus line, conga line, firing line,

     Caleb Spalding Atwood

gold mine, grapevine, hot line, land mine, mine, moonshine, pine, pipeline, porcupine, punch line, salt mine, silver mine, shrine, sparkling wine, strip mine, swine, trap line, trotline, turbine, turpentine, valentine, wine

Homing Pigeon: carrier pigeon, clay pigeon, passenger pigeon, religion, stool pigeon

Honey Badger: nil

Honeybee: See Bee.

Hoot Owl: see Barn Owl

Horned toad: abode, area code, bar code, boatload, commode, dress code, Morse code, mother lode, payload, penal code, railroad, trainload, tree toad, wagon load, zip code

Hornet: hair net

Horse: divorce, golf course, work force

Horsefly: see Butterfly

Horseshoe Crab: black lab, cab, tab, taxicab

Hound: see Basset Hound.

Hummingbird: see Bird

Humpback Whale: Airedale, brail, coattail, cocktail, cocktail, cottontail, e-mail, fairytale, ginger ale, hangnail, jail, junk mail, killer whale,

monorail, nail mail, nail, nightingale, pigtail, pilot whale, ponytail, pygmy whale,
quail, sail, scale, snail, snail mail, sperm
whale, tattletale, vapor trail, veil, voicemail,
beluga whale

Husky: See Bee.

Hyena: arena, ballerina, cantina, javelina, marina,
                  subpoena

I RHYMING QUIP OPTIONS

Ibex: duplex, hex, index, spandex, sex, Tex-Mex,
                  texts, vex, wrecks

Ibis: bliss, hiss, kiss, miss, Swiss

Iguana: Americana, Botswana, fauna, marijuana,
                  prima donna, Nirvana, sauna

Impala: Guatemala, Kampala, koala, Valhalla

Inchworm: see Angleworm

Insect: architect, benign neglect, defect, halo ef-
                  fect, murder suspect, suspect

Irish Setter: chain letter, debtor, English setter, fan let-
                  ter, go-getter, jet-setter, newsletter, pace-
                  setter

J RHYMING QUIP OPTIONS

Jackal:	debacle, tackle, tabernacle debacle
Jackass:	bass, bluegrass, brass, class, magnifying glass, shot glass, teargas
Jackrabbit:	abbot, riding habit
Jaguar:	bar, car, bizarre, boxcar, bumper car, crowbar, freight car, gar, guitar, sitar, police car, squad car, wrecking bar
Javelina:	arena, ballerina, cantina, hyena, marina, subpoena
Jay:	ash tray, attaché, ballet, beret, bidet, blue jay, bouquet, cabaret, cabernet, café, chalet, Chevrolet, croquet, flight pay, hair spray, jay, manta ray, moray, negligee, Nene, osprey, pepper spray, sleigh, stingray, subway, toupee, Valentine's day
Jellyfish:	see Angelfish
June bug:	see Bed Bug

K RHYMING QUIP OPTIONS

Kangaroo	Rat: bat, cat, gat, hat, spat, vat
Kangaroo:	barbecue, brew, canoe, caribou, cockatoo, cork screw, ewe, gnu, hairdo, horse shoe,

igloo, IOU, kangaroo, kazoo, micro brew, shampoo, tattoo, tofu, voodoo, Waterloo

Killer Bee:	See Bee.
Killer Whale:	see Airedale
King Bird:	see Bird
King Cobra:	nil
King Crab:	black lab, cab, fiddler crab, flab
King Fisher:	nil
King Salmon:	backgammon, famine
King Snake:	see Coral Snake
Kingfish:	see Angelfish
Kit Fox:	see Fox
Kitten:	Britton, flea-bitten, mitten, snake-bitten
Kiwi:	see Bee.
Koala:	Guatemala
Kodiak:	backpack, blackjack, bootblack, bric-a-brac, Cadillac, cognac, diamondback, gunnysack, hatchback, ice pack, gunny sack, hatchback, heart attack, kayak, knapsack, Muzak, Prozac, racetrack, silverback, racetrack, razorback, setback, six-pack, ski rack, smokestack, tarmac, thumbtack, tie rack, yak

          Caleb Spalding Atwood

Koi: boy, busboy, cowboy, decoy, poi, envoy,
                        ploy, tinker toy

Komodo Dragon: bandwagon, battlewagon, chuck wagon,
                        Conestoga wagon, covered wagon, paddy
                        wagon, snapdragon, station wagon

L RHYMING QUIP OPTIONS

Labrador: ambassador, bed sore, boar, book store,
                        commodore, condor, cuspidor, drug store,
                        fire door, humidor, liquor store, man-o-
                        war, matador, mentor, memoir, oar, par-
                        quet floor, picador, pinafore, raptor,
                        realtor, revolving door, saddle sore, storm
                        door, swinging door, toreador, troubadour,
                        war

Ladybug: see Bed Bug

Lake Trout: see Brook Trout

Lamb: battering ram, cardiogram, clam, exam,
                        grand slam, hologram, lamb, monogram,
                        mammogram, ram, scam, sky cam, spam,
                        telegram, tinker's damn, traffic jam, web
                        cam

Lamprey: See Bee

Lap Dog: see Dog

Largemouth Bass: see Bass

Lark: amusement park, aardvark, ballpark, Cutty Sark, Deutschemark, ear mark, lark, Makers Mark, meadowlark, monarch, narc, national park, shark, skylark, theme park, tiger shark

Leech: beech, breach, bleach, each, speech, impeach, Long Beach, Palm Beach, Myrtle Beach, Newport Beach, Daytona Beach, Huntington Beach, Miami Beach, Omaha Beach, peach, Virginia Beach

Lemming: G-string, hamstring, shoestring, sing, sling, teething ring.

Lemon Shark: see Aardvark

Lemon Sole: see Dover Sole

Lemur: creamer, femur, reamer, schemer, screamer, steamer, streamer, blasphemer, daydreamer, redeemer

Leopard Seal: see Cockatiel

Leopard: see German Shepherd

Lhasa Apso: nil

Lice: mice, sacrifice, thin ice

Lightning Bug: see Bed Bug

Ling: see Gosling

Lion fish: see Angelfish

          Caleb Spalding Atwood

Lion: Hawaiian, Paraguayan, Uruguayan, scion

Lipizzaner: medal of honor

Lizard: blizzard, gizzard, wizard

Llama: Brahma, drama, mama, Bahamas, pajama,
                 Dalai Lama, docudrama, melodrama, pa-
                 norama, photodrama, psychodrama, Yoko-
                 hama

Lobster: mobster

Locust: blind trust, wanderlust

Longhorn: see Bighorn

Loon: see Baboon

Louse: see Deer Mouse

Love Bird: see Bird

Lynx: drinks, jinx

M RHYMING QUIP OPTIONS

Macaw: Arkansas, attorney at law, band saw, bear
                 claw, blue law, brother-in-law, buzz saw,
                 bylaw, chaw, chainsaw, civil law, claw,
                 coleslaw, coping saw, daughter-in-law, fa-
                 ther-in-law, flaw, jaw, jigsaw, keyhole saw,
                 law, lockjaw, Mackinac, mother-in-law,
                 Murphy's Law, Omaha, Panama, paw, raw,

ripsaw, saber saw, Saginaw, scofflaw, see-
saw, Shah, son-in-law, southpaw, straw,
squaw, Utah, whipsaw, Wichita

Mackerel: horse mackerel, king mackerel

Maggot: aeronaut, astronaut.

Magpie: see Butterfly

Mahi-mahi: nil

Mako Shark: see Aardvark

Malamute: birthday suit, boot, cheroot, crapshoot,
deaf mute, flute, galoot, G suit, hip boot,
jumpsuit, leisure suit, pantsuit, parachute,
snowsuit, spacesuit, sweat suit, swim suit,
track suit, trade route, zootsuit,

Mallard: armed guard, backyard, bard, barnyard,
blowhard, bodyguard, bone yard, business
card, Christmas card, color guard, credit
card, farmyard, graveyard, honor guard,
ID card, junkyard, leotard, lifeguard,
petard, Saint Bernard, scorecard, video
card, wild card

Mamba: Viola de Gemba, Samba

Manatee: see Bee.

Man-o-war: see Boar

Manta ray: see Blue jay

    Caleb Spalding Atwood

Mare: see Bear

Marlin: see Emperor Penguin

Marmoset: barrette, chess set, cigarette, clarinet, cold sweat, coronet, Corvette, fish net, jet set, roulette, base hit, drill bit, snake pit, stock split, tar pit, tourniquet

Martin: bathtub gin, bin, bobby pin, cave in, chin, clothespin, coonskin, cotton gin, drive in, fin, firing pin, gin, hairpin, grin, Looney bin, pigskin, safety pin, Simian, sin, spin, tin, violin

Maverick: see Chick

Mayfly: see Butterfly

Meadowlark: see Aardvark

Meer Kat: bat, cat, gat, hat, rat, spat, vat

Milk Snake: air brake, backache, bellyache, birthday cake, coffee break, disc brake, earthquake, emergency brake, fruitcake, garter snake, green snake, grubstake, hand brake, king snake, parking brake, rattlesnake, sea snake, snake, snow flake, tax break, wedding cake see Coral Snake

Millipede: bead, birdseed, chicken feed, centipede, duckweed, hayseed, millipede, nosebleed, poppy seed, screed, seaweed, stampede

Mink:	cuff link, drink, ice rink, ink, kitchen sink, mixed drink, red ink, rinky-dink, shrink, sink
Minnow:	air show, art deco, backhoe, bronco, buffalo, bungalow, cash flow, cello, chapeau, chateau, crossbow, crow, doe, dog and pony show, domino, echo, escrow, free throw, gazebo, halo, hoe, inferno, longbow, mango, minnow, mistletoe, mosquito, oboe, Oleo, Oreo, peep show, piccolo, radio, rainbow, rhino, rodeo, scarecrow, ski tow, skid row, sparrow, standing O, stereo, tennis elbow, TKO, trousseau, volcano, widow
Mockingbird:	bluebird, buzzword, crossword, hummingbird, mockingbird, password, redbird, swearword, Thunderbird, whirlybird, jailbird
Mole:	bankroll, beanpole, bedroll, bowl, charcoal, coal, goal, charcoal, cruise control, dust bowl, field goal, fishbowl, fishing pole, flag pole, foal, fox hole, hellhole, loophole, opinion poll, payroll, peephole, pothole, rock and roll, ski patrol, ski pole, south pole, super bowl, toll, totem pole, washbowl
Mongoose:	deuce, goose juice, moose, noose, Zeus

Caleb Spalding Atwood

Monkey:	see Bee.
Moose:	abuse, caboose, calaboose, fruit juice, juice, masseuse, goose, mongoose, noose, papoose, produce, prune juice, snow goose
Moray Eel:	automobile, bookmobile, buffing wheel, cockatiel, curb appeal, eel, elephant seal, Ferris wheel, flywheel, glockenspiel, harp seal, leopard seal, paddle wheel, seal, spinning wheel, stiletto heel
Mosquito Hawk:	crock, frock, hemlock, wok
Mosquito:	burrito, veto
Moth:	broth, breechcloth, cloth, drop cloth, face cloth, loincloth, sloth, tablecloth, washcloth
Mountain Goat:	see Angora Goat
Mountain lion:	Hawaiian, Paraguayan, Uruguayan, scion
Mourning Dove:	baseball glove, boxing glove
Mouse:	alehouse, beach house, blouse, bunkhouse, clubhouse, deer mouse, dog house, doll house, dormouse, field mouse, flophouse, grouse, guardhouse, hen house, jailhouse, lighthouse, louse, opera house, penthouse, slaughter house, smokehouse, statehouse, titmouse
Mudpuppy:	yuppie

Mule:	barstool, carpool, cathouse, correspondence school, fool, footstool, fuel, school, grade school, grammar school, home school, Liverpool, medical school, motor pool, nursery school, parochial school, reform school, senior high school, summer school, synfuel, toadstool, tire tool, van pool, vestibule, whirlpool
Musk ox:	fox, socks, stocks
Muskrat:	see Alley Cat
Musky:	see Husky
Mussel:	bustle, muscle
Mustang:	boomerang, chain gang, fang, gang, road gang
Myna Bird:	see Bird

N RHYMING QUIP OPTIONS

Nanny goat:	see Angora Goat
Needlefish:	see Angelfish
Nene"	see Bee.
Neon Tetra:	baccarat, chutzpah, et cetera, spa,
Newt:	see Malamute

     Caleb Spalding Atwood

Night crawler: brawler, dollar, fire baller, footballer, hauler, knuckleballer, mauler, pub crawler, squalor, trawler

Night hawk: see fish hawk

Nightingale: see Airedale

O RHYMING QUIP OPTIONS

Ocelot: aquanaut, astronaut, big shot, blind spot, blood clot, blot, buckshot, chamber pot, cheap shot, clot, coffeepot, cosmonaut, cot, despot, dreadnaught, dunk shot, feedlot, fox-trot, gunshot, jackpot, juggernaut, knot, mascot, melting pot, moon shot, mug shot, parking lot, patriot, penalty shot, polka dot, pot, robot, slap shot, slingshot, slipknot, sunspot, teapot, tot, touch-me-not, turkey trot, yacht

Octopus: glamour-puss, platypus, puss, schuss, sour-puss

Opossum: blossom

Orangutan: afghan, anchorman, ape-man, bedpan, clan, fan, frogman, family man, frying pan, hatchet man, Iran, Japan, mailman, news-man, oilcan, oilman, ombudsman, Pilt-down man, plan, sampan, saucepan, snowman, superman

Orca:	aorta
Oriole:	see Mole
Osprey:	see Blue Jay
Ostrich:	bait and switch, drainage ditch, fast-pitch, jock itch, kitsch, perfect pitch, rich, sales pitch, slow-pitch, snitch, switch, timber hitch, toggle switch, witch, wild pitch
Otter:	alma mater, blotter, boycotter, firewater, flyswatter, globe-trotter, groundwater, hot water, ice water, rainwater, saltwater, sea otter, soda water, squatter, tap water, teeter-totter, wastewater, whitewater
Owl:	barn owl, beach towel, crying towel, night owl, screech owl, snowy owl, tea towel, trowel, Turkish towel, waterfowl
Owlet:	see Eaglet
Ox:	see Fox
Oyster:	nil

P RHYMING QUIP OPTIONS

Packrat:	see Alley Cat
Palomino:	Angelino, bambino, cappuccino, casino, concertino

    Caleb Spalding Atwood

Panda:	memoranda, propaganda, Uganda, veranda
Panther:	nil
Parakeet:	aquavit, athlete, beet, bed sheet, biathlete, box seat, cheat, cheat sheet, cold feet, crib sheet, deadbeat, decathlete, drumbeat, easy street, elite, hot seat, jump seat, potty seat, prickly heat, pink sheet, rap sheet, retreat, skeet, spreadsheet, suite, swap meet, Wall Street
Parrot:	see Ferret
Partridge:	auction bridge, bridge, contract bridge, footbridge, ridge, fridge, suspension bridge
Peacock:	see Croc
Peahen:	see Guinea Hen
Peccary:	see Calamari
Pekinese:	see Bees
Pelican:	bullpen, comedienne, den, five-and-ten, fountain pen, playpen, poison pen, RN
Penguin:	gin, bobby pin, cave-in, clothespin, coonskin, cotton gin, dustbin, gin, hairpin, pigskin, Ritalin, rolling pin, safety pin, sea urchin, sheepskin, sloe gin, tenpin, violin
Perch:	church, research, strip search.
Peregrine:	see Dolphin

Pheasant: birthday present, present

Pig: see Guinea Pig

Pigeon: see Carrier Pigeon

Piglet: see Marmoset

Pike: see Northern Pike

Pilot Fish: see Angelfish

Pilot Whale: see Airedale

Pinto: see Bronco

Piranha: Botswana, fauna, prima donna, Americana

Pit Bull: see Bull

Platypus: puss

Polar bear: see Bear

Polecat: alley cat, bat, cat, gat, hat, rat, spat, vat

Pollywog: see Birddog

Pomeranian: Albanian, Jordanian, Lithuanian, Panaman-
                     ian, Pennsylvanian, Tanzanian, Ukrainian

Pompano: piano, soprano

Pony: see Abalone

Poodle: apple strudel, doodle, kit and caboodle

Porcupine: see Holstein

Porpoise: nil

Possum: see Black Drum

Prairie Chicken: see Chicken

Prairie Dog: see Birddog

Prawn: see Fawn

Praying Mantis: Atlantis

Pronghorn: see Bighorn

Puff adder: extension ladder, fish ladder, step ladder

Puffin: muffin

Pug: see Bed Bug

Pullet: see Eaglet

Puma: Montezuma

Puppy: see Guppy

Purple Finch: see Finch

Pygmy Goat: see Angora goat

Pygmy Owl: see Barn Owl

Pygmy Whale: see Airedale

Python: see Prawn

Q RHYMING QUIP OPTIONS

Quahog: see Birddog

Quail: see Airedale

Quarter Horse: see Horse

Quetzal: cabal, canal, corral, decal

R RHYMING QUIP OPTIONS

Rabbit: abbot, cohabit, habit

Raccoon: see Baboon

Racehorse: see Arabian Horse

Rainbow Trout: see Brook Trout

Ram: battering ram, cardiogram, clam, exam, grand slam, hologram, lamb, monogram, mammogram, ram, scam, sky cam, spam, telegram, tinker's damn, traffic jam, web cam

Raptor: see Albacore

Rat: see bat

Rattlesnake: see Coral Snake

Raven: bull pen, carcinogen, cayenne, comedienne, den, five and ten, fountain pen, men, playpen, poison pen, RN

                  Caleb Spalding Atwood

Razorback:	see Diamondback
Red Panda:	see Giant Panda
Red Snapper:	kidnapper, scrapper, trapper, whippersnapper, wire tapper, wrapper
Redbird:	see Bird
Redfish:	see Angelfish
Reebok:	see Croc
Reef Shark:	see Aardvark
Reindeer:	see Deer
Rhino:	see Bronco
Ribbon Fish:	see Angelfish
Ridley Turtle:	see Box Turtle
River Otter:	see Otter
Robin:	see Dolphin
Rock Bass:	see ass
Rock Lobster:	see Lobster
Rockfish:	see Angelfish
Rodent:	cement, convent, detent, pup tent, regiment, rubber cement, vice president
Rooster:	see Bantam Rooster
Rottweiler:	nil

S RHYMING QUIP OPTIONS

Sable: cable, fable, gale, label, round table, stable, table, timetable, turntable

Sailfish: see Angelfish

Saint Bernard: see Mallard

Salamander: see Gander

Salmon: Atlantic Salmon, King Salmon, famine

Sand Dollar: collar, flea collar, white-collar

Sand Fly: see Butterfly

Sand Hill Crane: see Great Dane

Sandpiper: diaper, entrepreneur, restaurateur, saboteur, spur

Sardine: acetylene, caffeine, canteen, E-zine, gangrene, guillotine, Halloween, latrine, limousine, magazine, marine, morpheme, nicotine, pinball machine, putting green, queen, ravine, screen, slot machine, smokescreen, spleen, submarine, trampoline, Vaseline, washing machine, wolverine

Savannah Cat: see Alley Cat

Sawfish: see Angelfish

Scallop: nil

Schnauzer:	carouser, rabble rouser, trouser, web browser
Schnook:	coloring book, comic book, fry cook, pastry cook, telephone book
Scorpion:	nil
Scotty:	See Bee.
Scrod:	see Cod
Sea anemone:	See Bee.
Sea Bass:	see Ass
Sea Cow:	see Cow (no pun intended)
Sea Eagle:	see Beagle
Sea Hawk:	see Fish Hawk
Sea Lion:	see Lion (no pun intended)
Sea Otter:	see Otter
Sea Slug:	see Bed Bug
Sea Snake:	see Coral Snake
Sea Trout:	see Brook Trout
Sea Urchin:	see Dolphin
Seagull:	see Gull
Seahorse:	see Arabian Horse
Seal:	see Cockatiel

Seeing Eye Dog: see Birddog

Shad: see Crawdad

Shark: see Aardvark

Sheep Dog: see Birddog

Sheep: barkeep, chimney sweep, creep, jeep, rubbish heap, scrap heap, trash heap, veep

Shellfish: see Angelfish

Sheltie: see Bee

Shetland Pony: see Abalone

Shrew: see Caribou

Shrimp: blimp, imp, wimp

Siamese Cat: see Angora Cat

Sidewinder: binder, coffee grinder, fact finder, meat grinder, organ grinder

Silkworm: see Angleworm

Silver Fox: see Fox

Silverback: see Diamondback

Skink: drink, fink, shrink, stink, wink, zinc

Skunk: see Chipmunk

Skylark: see Aardvark

Sloth: see Moth

   Caleb Spalding Atwood

Slug:	see Bed Bug
Smelt:	conveyor belt, corn belt, fan belt, garter belt, money belt, seat belt
Snail Darter:	barter, charter, garter, kick-starter
Snail:	see Airedale
Snake:	see Coral Snake
Snapping Turtle:	see Box Turtle
Snipe:	bagpipe, hype, pitch pipe, stovepipe, tailpipe
Snow Goose:	see Canadian Goose
Snow Leopard:	see German Shepherd
Snowshoe Hare:	see Bear
Snowy Owl:	see Barn Owl
Sockeye:	see Firefly
Sow:	see Cow
Sparrow:	see Bronco
Speckled Trout:	see Brook Trout
Sperm Whale:	see Airedale
Spider Monkey:	see Capuchin Monkey
Spider:	see Black Widow Spider
Spoonbill Cat:	see Angora Cat

Spring Chicken: see Chicken

Springbok: see Croc

Springer Spaniel: see Brittany Spaniel

Squid: see Giant Squid

Squirrel: ball girl, bat girl, Campfire girl, chorus girl, cover girl, cowgirl, girl, flower girl, flying squirrel, mother-of-pearl, mural, pearl, pin curl, pinup girl, playgirl, Squirrel, sweater girl

Stag: beanbag, body bag, doggie bag, dog tag, flag, jet lag, price tag, punching bag, saddle bag, sandbag, toe-tag, tote bag

Stallion: battalion, Italian, medallion

Starfish   see Angelfish

Starling   see Duckling

Steelhead   see Copperhead

Steenbok   see Croc

Steer   see Deer

Stingray   see Blue jay

Stinkbug   see Bedbug

Stork   cork, fork, New York, pitchfork, salad fork, tuning fork

   Caleb Spalding Atwood

Sturgeon	surgeon, plastic surgeon, surgeon, virgin
Sunfish	see Angelfish
Swallow	Apollo, Sao Paulo
Swan	see Prawn
Swine	see Porcupine
Swordfish	see Angelfish

T RHYMING QUIP OPTIONS

Tabby Cat:	see Angora Cat
Tadpole:	see Foal
Tapeworm:	see Angleworm
Tapir:	see Deer
Tarantula"	nil
Tarpon"	see Atlantic Salmon
Tasmanian Devil:	bedevil, dishevel, level, revel, bevel, bi-level, daredevil, entry-level, level, sea level, split level
Teal:	see Cockatiel
Termite:	bagpipe, blight, bombsight, box kite, bullfight, campsite, cellulite, cockfight, cockfight, dogfight, dynamite, firefight,

flashlight, fleabite, floodlight, frostbite, gunfight, headlight, kite, lamplight, limelight, meteorite, moonlight, overbite, parasite, penlight, pilot light, prizefight, satellite, searchlight, skylight, spaceflight, spotlight, stalagmite, stalactite, traffic light, torchlight, web site

Terrapin: see Dolphin

Terrier: derriere

Tic: see Chick

Tiger Shark: see Aardvark

Tiger Shrimp: see Shrimp

Tiger: Bengal Tiger, hang glider, saber toothed tiger, Siberian tiger

Tilapia: see Nutria

Timber Wolf: see Gray Wolf

Titmouse: see Deer Mouse

Toad: see Horned Toad

Tomcat: see Alley Cat

Tortoise: see Ibis

Toucan: see Doberman

Toy Fox Terrier: see Fox Terrier

                  Caleb Spalding Atwood

Tree Frog:	see Birddog
Tree Swallow:	see Swallow
Tree Toad:	see Horned Toad
Triggerfish:	see Angelfish
Trout:	see Brook Trout.
Trumpeter Swan:	see Fawn
Tsetse Fly:	see Butterfly
Tuna:	Montezuma, puma, vicuna
Turkey Vulture:	see Black Vulture
Turkey:	see Bee
Turtle Dove:	see Dove
Turtle:	Crepe myrtle, wax myrtle, loggerhead turtle, Ridley turtle, snapping turtle

U RHYMING QUIP OPTIONS

Nil.

V RHYMING QUIP OPTIONS

| Varmint: | blueprint, fingerprint, lint, mint, newsprint, skinflint, wind sprint |

Vicuna:	see Tuna
Viper:	bagpiper, diaper, sniper
Vole:	see Foal
Vulture:	agriculture, aquaculture, aviculture, culture, counterculture, horticulture, viniculture

W RHYMING QUIP OPTIONS

Wallaby:	See Bee.
Walleye:	see Fly.
Walrus:	airbus, blunderbuss, bus, minibus, school bus, surplus
Wapiti:	See Bee.
Warthog:	see Birddog
Wasp:	nil
Watchdog:	see Birddog
Water Beetle:	nil
Water Buck:	see Buck
Water Buffalo:	see Bronco
Water Moccasin:	see Dolphin
Weasel:	easel, diesel, measles

     Caleb Spalding Atwood

Weevil: upheaval

Whale: see Airedale Beluga Whale

Whippet: banana split, bit, cockpit, culprit, counter-
                     feit, grit, hypocrite, obit, pulpit, tar pit,
                     snake pit

Whip-poor-Will: see Bluegill

White Bass: see Ass

White Shark: see Aardvark

White Tailed Deer: see Deer

Whitefish: see Angelfish

Whiting: see Herring

Wild Boar: see Albacore

Wildcat: see Alley Cat

Wildebeest: far east, feast, yeast

Wirehaired Terrier: see Fox Terrier

Wolf pack: see Diamondback

Wolf: gray wolf, timber wolf

Wolverine: Sardine, Submarine,

Wombat: see alley cat

Woodchuck: see Buck

Woodcock: see Croc

Woodpecker:	double-decker, exchequer, fact-checker, rubbernecker, wrecker
Worm:	see Angleworm
Wren:	see Guinea Hen

X RHYMING OPTIONS

Nil

Y RHYMING OPTIONS

Yak:	see Diamondback
Yellow Jacket:	numbers racket, pay packet, racquet, squash racket, tennis racket
Yellow Lab:	black lab, crab, flab, king crab, stab

Z RHYMING OPTIONS

| Zebra: | Nil. |

APPENDIX C

VERB OPTIONS

These 88 verbs can be employed with the aforementioned 172 pivots and 646 pegs to create 9,777,856 Quips. Tack on two of each and the total exceeds 10 million and should suffice.

Accumulate / ache for / admire / allow / adore / amass / amuse / annoy / applaud / appreciate / baffle / believe / boss / care for / caress / cater to / chase / cherish / cling to / coddle / collect / confide in / covet / crave / cuddle / damage / delight / depend upon / deserve / desire / dote on / dream of / embrace / enchant / esteem / exalt / fancy / fondle / gather / guard / greet / hail / haunt / hug / hunger for / hunt / idolize / itch for / kick / laud / like / lionize / long for / love / miss / need / nurture / obey / pamper / praise / pray for / prize / promise / promote / protect / ravish / regale / relish / rely on / require / respect / yearn for / revel in / revere / savor / seek / stockpile / swear by / thrill / treasure / unite / value / visit / want / weep for / welcome / worship.

These 88 verbs can be employed with the afore mentioned 172 pivots and 646 pegs in Appendixes A & B to create 9,777,856 Quips. Add five more of each and your total will eclipse ten million – to i.e.10,410,400.

                    Caleb Spalding Atwood